Joshua A. Klein
Editor-in-Chief
Designer

Michael Updegraff
Editorial Assistant

Jim McConnell
Content Editor

Megan Fitzpatrick
Content & Copy Editor

———————————————

© 2018 *Mortise & Tenon Magazine*

All rights reserved. No part of this publication may be reproduced in any form or by any means including electronic and mechanical methods, without prior written permission from the publisher, except in the case of brief quotations in critical reviews and certain noncommercial uses permitted by copyright law.

Send all inquiries to:
info@mortiseandtenonmag.com

To subscribe, visit:
www.mortiseandtenonmag.com

Mortise & Tenon Magazine
14 Porcupine Ln
Sedgwick, ME 04676

Printed in the United States of America

ISSUE FIVE

10   10,000 Hours: A Journey into Japanese Woodworking
       KIM CHOY

24   Convergent Design: The Six-board Viking Sea Chest
       KATE FOX

36   An Unlikely Masterpiece: Examining Chester Cornett's Bookcase Rocking "Chire"
       BRENDAN GAFFNEY

50   Coopering: A Harsh Mistress
       MARSHALL SCHEETZ

66   Tools for Learning: Woodworking with Young Children
       JOSHUA A. KLEIN & MICHAEL UPDEGRAFF

80   Woodworking in Classic Literature
       MEGAN FITZPATRICK

90   Examination of an 18th-century Mahogany Tea Table

100   An Overwhelming Call: The Life & Work of Eric Sloane
       MICHAEL UPDEGRAFF

112   In Tight Quarters: A Conversation with Spencer Nelson About Apartment Woodworking

122   Hand in Hand with Jonathan Fisher: Interacting with the Legacy of a Rural Artisan
       JOSHUA A. KLEIN

139   Book Recommendation: *Oak Furniture: The British Tradition*
       DEREK OLSON

CONTRIBUTORS

Kim Choy is a furniture craftsman based in Singapore. He is largely self-taught and is always on a pursuit to learn woodworking techniques from different regions. He believes in a wide spectrum of woodworking where there should be no boundaries, with many traditions and cultures to learn from. Kim makes contemporary furniture with hand tools to honor these traditions. www.shibuifurniture.co

Kate Fox is a combat veteran who has found a new purpose and passion in life through woodworking. Schooled in fine furniture making at Gary Rogowski's Northwest Woodworking Studio, where she now teaches, her obsession is studying woodcraft techniques from various ancient cultures and enjoying their recreation. A native Oregonian, she lives in her beloved yurt in the foothills of the Cascade range where she writes about, creates with, and plans the teaching of hand-tool woodworking. Her ultimate goal is to open her own modest school in the Cascades where she can host classes for veterans and youths. www.woodshrew.com

Brendan Bernhardt Gaffney is a woodworker, teacher, and writer based in Covington, Kentucky. After learning cabinetmaking from his father (and a stint in academia designing and researching musical instruments), he attended College of the Redwoods (now The Krenov School) where he honed his talents as a designer and maker of fine furniture. Since attending school, Brendan has worn the hats of toolmaker, teacher, writer, and furniture maker, building everything from ancient rulers, geometers' tools, gallery furniture, and greenwood chairs. He has been published in *Popular Woodworking* and *Mortise & Tenon* magazines. Currently, he is researching and building vernacular chair designs from around the world and writing a biography of James Krenov to be published by Lost Art Press in 2020. www.burn-heart.com

Marshall Scheetz is a practicing cooper based in Williamsburg, Virginia, where he lives with his wife and two children. He served a six-year apprenticeship under a traditional master cooper. Inspired by historical research, he practices tight, dry, and white coopering, and creates accurate reproductions of period cooperage including hogsheads, barrels, firkins, canteens, butter churns, tubs, piggins, and buckets, along with artwork inspired by the trade. Marshall is a historian and researches the cooper's trade with an emphasis on the 18th and 19th centuries. Collaboration with researchers, archaeologists, curators, and other tradesmen furthers his understanding about the art and science of coopering and coopered containers. He is owner of Jamestown Cooperage, found at www.jamestowncooperage.com.

Joshua A. Klein is editor-in-chief of *Mortise & Tenon Magazine* and has been published by *American Period Furniture* and *Popular Woodworking Magazine*. Joshua has been selected every year since 2015 for the Early American Life Directory of Traditional American Crafts for his hand-tool-only approach to period furniture making. He is the author of *Hands Employed Aright: The Furniture Making of Jonathan Fisher (1768-1847)* published by Lost Art Press in 2018. Joshua, with his wife and three sons, is currently restoring a 200-year-old cape while homesteading on the coast of Maine, always with an eye to learn from his cultural heritage.

Michael Updegraff lives in the Maine woods with his wife and three children. His jack-of-all-trades working background includes time as a house carpenter, sternman on a lobster boat, maker of custom canoe and kayak paddles, and 10 years as a yacht carpenter, varnisher, and rigger. Besides loving his editorial, customer service, and videography work for *M&T*, he enjoys running mountain trails, making useful things from trees, and drinking good coffee on road trips. Otherwise, he is likely somewhere in the forest, bucking and splitting next winter's firewood supply.

Megan Fitzpatrick is the editor and publisher at Rude Mechanicals Press (www.rudemechanicalspress.com). She is also a woodworker, teacher of hand-tool woodworking classes at schools and workshops throughout the United States, and is a former editor and content director of *Popular Woodworking*. In her spare time, she's rehabbing a 1906 American four-square that was turned into apartments in the 1950s, turning it back into a single-family home. Someday, after she's done with the house (so possibly never), she plans to make period-appropriate furniture for every room. But she used to study Shakespeare – so she might just fill the place with joint stools instead. Megan is currently working on a book, titled *Shakespeare's Furniture*.

Spencer Nelson is a furniture maker and software engineer. He started working with wood in Brooklyn, New York in 2014, making furniture and carving spoons in a small, third-floor apartment. The constraints of working in a small apartment naturally pushed him toward traditional hand-tool woodworking, with a particular bent towards Japanese techniques. He now lives with his wife in Seattle, Washington.

Derek Olson runs the Oldwolf Workshop Studio in La Crosse, Wisconsin. On the surface he is a dedicated husband, father, and healthcare professional, but deep down he's obsessed with woodworking, tools, and furniture. He suffers from ABAD (Acute Book Acquisition Disorder) and supports that habit through freelance illustration, writing, and occasional furniture commissions. Other distractions include medieval reenactment, experimental archaeology, movies, replica prop making, photography, tabletop gaming, hiking, and comic books. He tracks his day-to-day projects on Instagram under @oldwolf_workshop with more in depth explorations at www.blog.oldwolfworkshop.com.

FROM THE EDITOR

> *"Once we have given up trying to create anything completely original out of wood, it is possible to see how the convergent designs found in woodworking tradition have been honed through thousands of years of human trial, error, and adaptation, to perfectly meet the needs of the maker."*
>
> – KATE FOX

The other day, my wife and I were on the beach at our favorite tucked-away coastal-Maine cove. After an invigorating swim, we walked up an outcropping of rock with a view of the ocean expanse to discover a glass bottle had been dashed against the rocks. Knowing that most visitors to this place are barefoot, we decided to pick up the pieces as best we could.

After placing the few large fragments into a plastic cup, we squinted to see the smaller shards illuminated by the bright sun amidst dull pebbles and sea grass. Once I recovered everything I could see, I stepped to the other side only to find I had overlooked handfuls of glass hidden in plain sight.

It's easy to think you've seen it all when the sun shines so brightly on your subject of study. But it wasn't until I changed my point of view that many other shards, lying at other angles to the sun, became visible. Sometimes it takes a new perspective to see the big picture.

I hope the articles in this issue will provide a fresh vantage point for you. Too often, we view our handcraft heritage from only one narrow perspective (say, 18th-century English cabinetmaking) and tend to think only in terms of what we're familiar with. We forget that there are thousands of other trades and traditions that have unique approaches to working with wood.

Many of the articles in this issue have been a long time coming. Mike and I maintain a growing list of ideas for future research and, as it happened, several emerged in this issue. Because we never force a unifying theme onto our authors but instead allow them to pursue their own passion, Issue Five has a rich diversity.

Moving between Marshall Scheetz's introduction to cooperage, two apartment-dwelling authors from opposite ends of the world both working in the Japanese tradition, a biographical sketch of Eric Sloane, and thoughts about woodworking with small children in one issue is like walking full circle to let the sun illuminate the bigger picture. In my mind, a broad perspective on handcraft is desperately needed in the 21st-century hand-tool renaissance.

May this issue kindle a fascination with these different facets of our woodcraft heritage.

Joshua A. Klein,
Editor

10,000 HOURS
A Journey into Japanese Woodworking

Kim Choy

Singapore is a country where land is scarce. Like most of the population, I live in an apartment building so when I began woodworking I had very limited space to set up shop. The only available area I could utilize was the common corridor in my apartment building, and I would set up a temporary workspace whenever I needed to. I did not actually have a bench – my primary working surface was usually a plank of substantial weight and size.

Most makers are familiar with the concept that it takes 10,000 hours of practice to master your craft. In my early days of learning, I remember frustration as I struggled to dimension a big piece of walnut that had cupped and twisted badly. Ten-thousand hours seemed a long ways away. I knew the quality of my joinery was poor, but I convinced myself that a full workbench with workholding options would improve my technique and make those joints tight. Building a proper Roubo bench became my focus.

I began working with the plank on sawhorses, and with some creative clamping, it became a solid surface. When I needed to chop mortises, I preferred to work lower, so I would drop the plank down onto blocks bringing the top about 6" off the ground. This allowed me to sit on the workpiece, making it less tiring than standing. Due to the lack of a vise, there were occasional awkward moments trying to balance both myself and the wood. But soon enough I learned to make it work.

As I planned my design for the Roubo workbench, I looked into upgrading and expanding my arsenal of tools as well. I knew the bench joinery was significantly larger than anything I had previously dealt with. The first item I added to the list was a big Japanese smoothing plane. When I saw videos of Japanese woodworkers making micron-thickness gossamer shavings, I was sold. I thought that with a plane like that, I would be able to conquer any type of wood without problem. The fact that the smoothing plane is the most revered tool in the world of Japanese woodworking only added to my fascination. I was inspired by a story of a man in Japan who left his hometown to be a shrine builder's apprentice. He had stopped sending letters to his parents, and they worried about him for years. One day, the parents received a package. Inside, with no explanation, was a translucent wood shaving, several feet long and full width. The parents were immediately assured of his success. The shaving made it clear that during his long absence, their son had been quietly honing his skills to mastery.

But apart from recognizing that Japanese planes are used with a pulling action rather than a pushing, I knew next to nothing about them. This made shopping for a Japanese plane a daunting task due of the lack of information and resources available – it took me almost two months to decide on one. I settled for a large smoothing plane with a 2-3/4" (70mm) wide blade. Little did I know how hard it would be to pull shavings with such a wide blade, not to mention the difficulty of sharpening it. I also purchased a set of five Japanese chisels and a variety of saws, and waited patiently for them to arrive.

Traditional Japanese woodworking resonated with me because there were many similarities with the way I worked in my corridor workshop. One such was the reliance on gravity, hands, and legs for workholding rather than a sturdy workbench and vises. I was so intrigued by this approach that I set aside my planned workbench project to focus instead on learning the techniques of this tradition. It quickly became clear that the Japanese craftsmen I studied were working much more gracefully than I was, but I consoled myself with the idea that it might be due to a difference in the quality of our tools, and awaited my shipment. When my tools finally arrived, I was excited to set up and get down to work. I pulled out a piece of figured walnut that was relatively flat and smooth from having been worked hard with my No. 5 jack plane. I thought all of that planing would finally be worth it, now that I could use a big Japanese smoothing plane to take it to a higher level of finish. I pulled the plane from the farthest end to the middle with confidence and force, ready to see thin shavings flying out. Instead, I tore out a huge chunk of wood where the grain reversed. My weeks of anticipation went downhill from there.

Subsequently, whenever I considered trying my hand at smoothing any piece of wood with the Japanese plane, there was a pervading sense of fear that the nightmare would happen again. I started to fall back to my jack plane and set the Japanese plane aside.

Fortunately, the chisels were more straightforward. The only time-consuming aspect was lapping the backs during sharpening. As the steel was rather hard, I resorted to using my #400-grit diamond plate and removed quite a lot of material. The Japanese chisels were indeed nicer to hold in my hands than my Western butt chisels, but edge retention was not noticeably superior. More roadblocks started to appear when learning to sharpen freehand. The bevel angle on the chisels got subsequently higher and higher to a point where they were crushing wood fibers instead of cutting or shearing them. My once torrid affair with Japanese tools was quickly cooling.

In my previous profession as a software developer, I learned that if I found myself fighting to implement a feature, it usually meant that I didn't understand the full scope of the framework. Drawing on that knowledge, it dawned on me that if the framework here was the tried-and-true Japanese methodology backed by the weight of tradition (which built, among other things, thousands of awe-inspiring shrines), it was obvious that the problem was my own lack of understanding. Despite my frustrations, I was still fixated on the idea of incorporating Japanese tools into my workflow, and so whenever I had bench time, I made a point to spend the last hour tinkering

with my Japanese plane. But tinkering turned out to be an ineffective way to learn, and I eventually realized that I needed to dive in headfirst.

Hand-tool woodworking in every tradition requires maintaining sharp edges. While I had no problem using sharpening jigs, I wanted to teach myself traditional freehand sharpening to understand its benefits. I quickly learned that I had underestimated the skills needed to sharpen a 70mm blade. In retrospect, sharpening a smaller plane would have made things easier for both me and my sharpening stones. In addition, Japanese plane blades are constructed differently than modern Western irons. They have high-carbon steel as the cutting edge, laminated with soft iron that forms the bulk of the body (such as in early Western planes). The steel is heat-treated to be quite hard for good edge retention, but that hardness can make sharpening (especially lapping the back) difficult. To solve this problem, the Japanese blacksmith hollows out the back of the blade using a scraper just before heat-treating; that leaves far less surface area to sharpen on a stone. I had no problems with this until, after repeated sharpenings, I eventually ran out of flat land on the back.

I learned that the hollow on the back of the blade, known as *urasuki*, has to be maintained with a flat perimeter around the edge. This maintenance involves two processes: *uradashi* (tapping the steel out with a hammer) and *uraoshi* (flattening). The first time a person does this, the fear can be paralyzing because poor technique can easily crack the blade due to the brittleness of the hardened steel. But if I was going to use these tools to their potential, along with learning how to sharpen my blade, I had to muster my courage to learn to do this.

During my first time tapping out, my worst fears came true – the edge of the blade cracked so badly that I had to use a bench grinder to remove a significant amount of steel. On the other hand, it was during this incident that I learned how to grind a bevel freehand, and after fixing the cracked blade, I got back to sharpening. Strangely enough, after all the care it took to bring the blade back to a usable state, I suddenly felt the connection. I was slowly developing the right sense to hold the blade in a comfortable way and was able to maintain the bevel flat with each stroke on the sharpening stone. The biggest satisfaction came the first time I lifted my blade to reveal an even sheen on the bevel, and I could once again see the beautiful lamination line. There is just something mesmerizing about this feature of Japanese blades.

Armed with greater confidence, I proceeded to condition the wooden body. Japanese plane bodies do not have flat soles, but instead, intentional hollows down the length. The main purpose of these hollows is to reduce friction and to make maintenance easier. Depending on their use, large jointer planes could have up to three or four hollows. I decided to set mine up as a smoother with only two areas of contact. This configuration allows the tool edge to be

the last point of contact with the wood surface. In the two months after my plane arrived, the humidity shift caused the wooden body to slightly warp, so I used my jack plane to flatten the sole. What I didn't immediately realize was that I opened up the mouth because of my carelessness in removing too much wood. Not yet understanding the relationship between a tight mouth and the cutting angle, I went ahead with the next step of creating the hollow in the sole with a big chisel and scraping plane.

I was discouraged to find that my experience planing did not improve even after all of this work. I was still getting tear-out on difficult grain, and shavings jammed in the throat constantly. However, I found that the plane worked beautifully on end grain, which was a completely different experience than my jack plane. That, at least, gave me some encouragement.

In subsequent months, my progress stagnated. The turning point finally came when I had a chance to make a trip to Japan. I'd managed to contact Genki Nishiyama, a woodworker based in Yokohama, who I had been following very closely because of his strong technical skills and sense of furniture design. My agenda for the visit was simple – to gain a deeper understanding of the use of Japanese tools, particularly the plane. Because I was self-taught, I needed some form of direction to feel confident that I was headed in the right way. I thought if I could experience for myself how Genki-san's tools felt and worked, that could become my point of reference.

I spent an afternoon in his workshop asking him a list of burning questions I had compiled. My mind was a sponge, absorbing everything Genki-san demonstrated. He let me try his planes and his sharpening station. This visit gave me the chance to experience firsthand how a sharp, well-tuned handplane felt.

Through Genki-san's recommendation, I visited a traditional tool shop in the northeastern part of Tokyo that specializes in high-quality woodworking tools. The visit was enriching, almost like a spiritual experience. I visited with the owner, Inoue-san, a very knowledgeable man who, besides selling tools to professionals and hobbyists, teaches woodworking at a nearby high school.

Before this visit, I purchased my woodworking tools online, so seeing and holding the tools like this was eye-opening. I told Inoue-san I was looking for a smaller plane and a dovetailing chisel, and over a cup of coffee he explained which tools would suit me based on my needs and my budget. After I settled on the plane and chisel that I wanted, Inoue-san asked if I was in a hurry to leave (I wasn't). He smiled and asked his wife to fetch him a pail of water. He led me to his sharpening station, took out a flat piece of iron plate (*kanna-ba*), sprinkled some baby (talcum) powder onto the plate, and added a few drops of water from the pail to form a paste. Inoue-san then started to lap the back of my newly purchased plane blade. I had never seen such a process before, and I paid very close attention to what he was doing. The lapping was done in a controlled motion with light strokes.

After each burst of lapping, Inoue-san would turn the blade over to inspect it for even flatness. The super-fine abrasive paste polished the back, revealing high spots. After his initial flatness inspection, the back of the blade showed a highly polished strip all the way across, except for one of the corners. I expected Inoue-san to bring out a coarse stone and start lapping away to remove more material; instead, he took out an anvil made of soft wrought iron and reached for his hammer. "*Uradashi!*" he said. All of a sudden, I understood why *uradashi* would be more efficient than removing material. Because of the laminated construction of the blade, tapping the soft iron on the bottom of the bevel creates an impact that pushes out the hard steel. The soft anvil provided good support for the blade and absorbed the hammer blows. Inoue-san alternated

between the *kanna-ba* and anvil several times before the back was entirely flat. He then showed me proper freehand sharpening techniques on both synthetic and natural stones.

    After returning to Singapore, I was able to rely on my recent experiences to correct the mistakes I'd been making with my woodworking techniques. I soon moved into my own apartment and dedicated a room to be my permanent workshop. I saw this move as a new start on my journey with using Japanese tools, which were finally feeling natural for me. Desiring proficiency, I decided to put away the Western tools that I was familiar with, and I even hid my stash of sandpaper out of sight. This immersion forced me to learn how to prepare a surface for finishing using only Japanese planes.

Continued on page 20

With such a steep learning curve, it may be difficult to understand why someone would decide to use Japanese tools. I didn't originally embark on this journey in search of the best tools or ways to work with wood, but studying this tradition has taken me deeper than I ever imagined it would. Although the tools appear simple, time and time again they've humbled and grounded me, demonstrating that there is always something to learn.

Many aspects of Japanese tools have remained unchanged for centuries, because there has been no need to improve upon their design. Saws, for example, still retain the long wooden handle wrapped with rattan, not because better handles are hard to make but because the philosophy of simple, minimalist design has become part of what the tool is all about. Gripping a Japanese saw comes naturally, and it is hard to find fault with the design. The long handle instinctively tells us that there's room for both hands, which is useful for long rips.

My minimalist workbench has seen me through most of my work and will continue to do so. I no longer yearn for that mighty Roubo workbench because I've come to appreciate a versatile, no-frills worksurface that is easy to make and maintain. I've grown and matured as a woodworker using mainly Japanese tools, though I refuse to call myself a Japanese woodworker. Although these tools have influenced me in terms of woodworking process, and have become a gateway into the world of Japanese culture and furniture design, I still think in terms of a wide spectrum of woodworking, with many traditions and cultures to learn from.

I believe I am still a few hundred hours shy of reaching 10,000, and although the journey is well underway, I can see that there is still so much to learn. ◆

CONVERGENT DESIGN

The Six-board Viking Sea Chest

Kate Fox

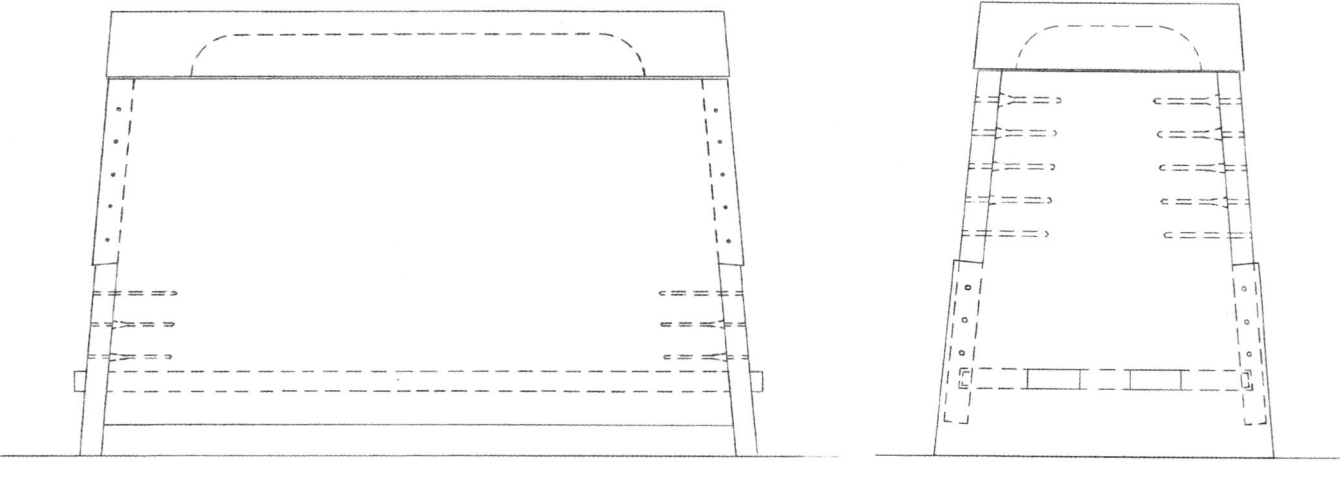

How many times have you heard it said, or lamented yourself, that nothing is original? At best it sounds cliché, at worst defeatist and cynical, but at the core of the statement is a golden nugget of truth that we should all learn to appreciate. As a modern woodworker I have often obsessed over a desire to design something original, but this is no small feat in a craft older than written history. I finally gave up on what seemed a futile expenditure of energy and turned my attention to examining how woodworking was done in the oldest examples I could find, only to realize that there was nothing original there, either.

It's a struggle most easily defined by terms found in other, more recent areas of study. In science the concept is called Multiple Discovery, wherein multiple scientists and inventors will simultaneously make the same, or very similar, discovery or invention.[1] Another model, termed Recombinant Conceptualization, predicates that every new concept is based off the melding of other pre-existing concepts.[2] Even biology has its own form of Multiple Discovery, a phenomenon known as Convergent Evolution, which occurs when distinct species independently develop analogous traits.

The concept of Multiple Discovery can easily be observed within the realm of woodworking. Human beings have been crafting solutions to our most basic needs from wood for thousands of years, spanning multiple eras of technology as experienced by multitudes of allopatric civilizations. Easily recognizable examples include inventions such as tripod stools, cross-framed chairs, A-frame structures, and round houses. The near-worldwide availability of wood as a practical building material, paired with its consistent constraints and capabilities, has led to many convergent design paths.

The six-board chest is another, albeit much lesser-known, example of convergent design. While most boxes and chests have six sides, "six-board chests" are identified as such not by the number of sides they have, but by the contradictory grain orientations of the front / back and side boards. The front, back, bottom, and lid all have horizontal grain orientation, while the sides run vertically, making them – as modern day woodworker Christopher Schwarz puts it – the "platypus of the woodworking world." Why is that so bizarre? Because they are made from wood, and wood as a building medium is subject to inevitable expansion and contraction alongside changes in humidity and temperature. Misaligned grain can cause cupping, twisting, and other problems. Because the components of these chests will shrink and expand constantly, and in different directions at the same time, this style of construction shouldn't actually work. Despite all this, many six-board chests have survived hundreds of years, and the construction style itself has persisted in popularity and utility for at least a thousand years. Examples of these chests have been found throughout multiple woodworking civilizations, and though many have tried to improve upon the design, the soundest version seems to also be the oldest. This Old Norse forebear of the six-board chest goes by few different names, predominately viking chest, sea chest, and 5° chest.

The oldest Norse sea chests discovered to date range from 900 A.D. to 1100 A.D., putting them soundly within the Viking Age, before friendly contact with Europe would begin to noticeably influence Old Norse technology and craft. These sea chests exhibited a few unique features not observed in the six-board chests being crafted in Europe at the same time. The most noticeable characteristic is the four inward-sloping sides, the reason for the 5° chest nickname. Of note, none of these chests had consistent 5° sloping corners, tending to range somewhere between 3° and 10° even within a single chest.

The Hedeby chest (Viking Age Norwegian, but also known as the Haithabu chest in modern German) is one of the earliest six-board sea chests discovered. It is unquestionably the author's favorite and has a story just as scandalous as its construction. It was found in pieces at the bottom of the Schlei inlet in modern-day Germany, a half-meter deeper in the mud than the famous viking ship Hedeby Wreck 1. When it was dumped over the edge of a different ship around 940 A.D., that section of inlet was the harbor of Hedeby, an important Scandinavian trading settlement during the Viking Era. The chest was found with the lock gouged out and a granite stone weighing it down. Most likely it was stolen, the contents forcibly removed, then the incriminating evidence was disposed of in the harbor.[3]

There is always a little hubbub around the label "viking," as many people think vikings were a people, which is not true. Viking is a verb, not a noun. The adventurers were Norse people, some of whom went raiding by sea, an activity referred to as viking. The Viking Age could more accurately be thought of as the Raiding Age of the Norse people. However, to call this a viking chest might not be entirely incorrect. There are theories that these chests were brought on longships to both serve as storage and seating for oarsmen and that the trapezoidal construction provided stability against both tipping and racking while traversing rough seas.[4] As with most theories about the Viking Age, with the complete lack of written history, this theory is mostly conjecture based on scant historical evidence and modern common sense. Another interesting attribute to the trapezoidal design of these chests and the oddly consistent size of three of the existing examples shows them to be of decent seat height and firmly stackable. So, if we are to believe that these sea chests were for taking on raiding trips, essentially making them campaign furniture similar to a modern soldier's footlocker, it would indeed be a (lower case) viking chest.

Consistent with this theory, the trapezoidal construction is apparent in all five chests dated to the Viking era (approximately 800 A.D. to just after the fall of Hedeby in 1066 A.D.) A gap in discoveries of any chests at all in Scandinavia spans from the 11th to 13th centuries, clouding these theories a bit, but from that point forward the medieval chests of the Norse lose their sloped sides for a more common rectilinear construction, presumably influenced by the six-board chests of continental Europe.

Even after conforming to the far less structurally sound (and arguably boring) 90° continental standard, Norse medieval chests still exhibit a couple of key joinery features that make them superior to other such chests. These include a notched butt joint at each corner, and mortise-and-tenon joinery solidly connecting the side boards to the bottom board. The bottom board and side boards do indeed match in their grain orientation. Connecting them at a slight angle and with a stout mortise and tenon creates a strong foundation, thus making the weakly aligned front and back boards unnecessary for the structural integrity of the chest.

To understand the reasoning behind the seemingly complicated construction of this chest requires looking back at the tools and methods available to the craftsman at the time, which were very different than those of the average modern woodworker. For instance, Scandinavian woodworkers didn't rely heavily on saws. Though available, they were mostly smaller handsaws intended for shorter cuts. Attempting long rip cuts would be tedious. Truing up the long grain on boards with an axe, however, would only take moments. (It is worth noting that the Europeans of the time did have excellent long saws, and chose to make chests in this fashion anyway.) Obviously, the Viking Age Norse did not use huge band saws to cut logs apart into boards as we do today. In fact, I dare say they likely would have seen this method as only capable of producing inferior lumber. Instead of using saws, which cut through wood fibers, creating weak runout spots along the way, they relied on various wedges to part logs along the grain into dimensional lumber.

This splitting technique is called riving, and from a straight-grained tree, these riven boards would exhibit exemplary strength and could be made thinner than sawn timber. This method of procuring lumber was key to the success of ocean-faring Norse viking ships and the subsequent expansion of the Norse people throughout the rest of the world.

Riving begins with a wedge and maul, splitting an appropriately straight-grained log into wedge-shaped boards right along a tree's natural growth lines. Using a variety of axes, adzes, and handplanes, a dimensional board can be shaped with annual growth rings perpendicular to the board face. This process is both labor- and skill-intensive, and produces more waste than medieval European and modern sawing methods, but there is no doubt that riven lumber was as close to perfect as a board could be made. The perpendicular alignment of the growth rings results in boards of excellent stability, where expansion and contraction would move consistently across a single plane, without cupping, bowing, or twisting. Cracking during drying was less likely, giving woodworkers the ability to safely build with green wood. Riven wood is also ideal for heat bending, as the intact fibers prevent blowout. The closest commercially milled cut achievable today is true quartersawn, which can still exhibit weak spots in the grain. This cut requires adjusting the log on the sawmill multiple times, and the trouble of the milling is reflected in the cost.

Despite all of the wonderful attributes of riven wood, it is not entirely without drawbacks. As with quartersawn timber, it is not possible to achieve a board of a width more than the radius of the tree itself, if that. The pith edge of a riven board tends to have more curvature and flaws along a much narrower thickness and will often require removal. To get a single radially riven board of 12" width you would have to source from a tree at least 30" in diameter – not a simple chore. The more twist the tree itself exhibits, the less flat boardage can be achieved. It is therefore paramount to be selective in choosing what tree you spend your time and energy on.

    The tree from which I sourced the boards for my recreation of this chest was more than adequate. Almost too much more, especially since it was my first large-scale riving project. A giant red oak had to be removed from a friend's yard after the three massive branches began to split the trunk downward from the crotch, endangering multiple homes. It required bringing in a crane and a full team of arborists to take down safely, and then the trunk was left behind for me to break my teeth on. It was an intimidatingly large log, 130" in circumference and 65" long. My hope was for rough-split boards approximately 20" wide.

    It was not an appealing project to begin with, as the splitting that had already naturally begun was in thirds, and every source I had researched specifically advised riving wood in halves to keep the pressure on each side of the wedges equal and thus keep the split centered. It took four days of hard labor, one friend with a chainsaw, a scissor-jack pinched from my '67 VW bug, lots of swear words, and a Costco bottle of ibuprofen, but at the end I had nine massive rough-split boards of red oak to take home for seasoning.

    Studying these 5'+ boards of oak and their wedge shape is what led me to the most exciting revelation I have made in this sea chest project. Many historians, Norse culture enthusiasts, and modern woodworkers have formed complex theories and argued vehemently about the reasoning behind the mysterious trapezoidal shape of the Norse sea chests. Some have proposed that the angled corners of the chest make it stronger than a 90° angle, or that these chests are all designed to a size that traveled well and possibly doubled for seating, but I think the earliest origins of the tapered design are much simpler; this is exactly the shape one would get from riving a single wedge-shaped board and trying through skill and design to build a chest while avoiding as much waste and extra labor as possible.

    I would argue that this frequently observed "design" developed not through choices based on aesthetics or intended uses, but through the parsimonious use of labor and resources often exhibited in old Norse crafts. This would have been a project easily taught by one woodworker to another through following a set order of operations, not needing any kind of written plan or adherence to measurements, and one that required only common tools of the trade in that time period.

I have now constructed a series of these chests from start to finish, in both period and modern fashions, and the consistent size of these chests suggests that they were likely constructed from single riven boards, of roughly the size that a woodworker was capable of felling, splitting, and handling alone. The perfect vertical grain of riven boards makes for satisfying building, because there is no fear that wood movement will pull one nailed face board away from another. It is a forgiving woodworking project, suitable even to those new at the trade.

Just because this form was historically constructed from a giant riven board does not mean that a similar effect can't be achieved with wood milled by an experienced sawyer. Even surly flat-sawn boards can be finessed into a successful and long-lasting sea chest.

There may even be some benefits to using flat-sawn lumber for this project. With the appropriate grain alignment and joinery, the natural cupping of the wood can be creatively utilized to enhance the structural stability of the chest, actually helping to hold it together during periods of wood movement. Additionally, using flat-sawn lumber can yield a larger chest than what has been seen in the historic, riven artifacts, because each board can reach up to the full diameter of the tree from which it was sourced.

There is truly no wrong way to create with wood (so long as you understand how it moves and plan your joinery accordingly), but when it comes to lasting designs, it is best to realize that there is nothing new under the sun. Once we have given up trying to create anything completely original out of wood, it is possible to see how the convergent designs found in woodworking tradition have been honed through thousands of years of human trial, error, and adaptation, to perfectly meet the needs of the maker. ◆

ENDNOTES

1. Robert K. Merton and Piotr Sztompka, *On Social Structure and Science* (Chicago: University of Chicago Press, 1996)
2. David Lamb and Susan M. Easton, *Multiple Discovery: The Pattern of Scientific Progress* (Amersham: Avebury, 1984)
3. Sven Kalmring, "Of Thieves, Counterfeiters and Homicides: Crime in Hedeby and Birka," *Fornvännen* 105, No. 4, 2010, 281-290
4. Detlev Ellmers, "Mit Seekiste und Bettzeug an Bord: das Reisegepäck der Seefahrenden vom Mittelalter bis zum frühen 20. Jahrhundert," *Hansische Geschichtsblätter* 127, 2009, 5

FURTHER REFERENCES

Schietzel, Kurt. *Spurensuche Haithabu: Archäologische Spurensuche in Der Frühmittelalterlichen Ansiedlung Haithabu; Dokumentation Und Chronik 1963 – 2013*. Neumünster: Wachholtz, 2013.

Roesdahl, Else, and David Wilson. *From Viking to Crusader: The Scandinavians and Europe, 800-1200*. Uddevalla, Sweden: Bohusläningens Boktryckeri, 1992.

Graham-Campbell, James. *The Viking World*. London: Frances Lincoln, 2013.

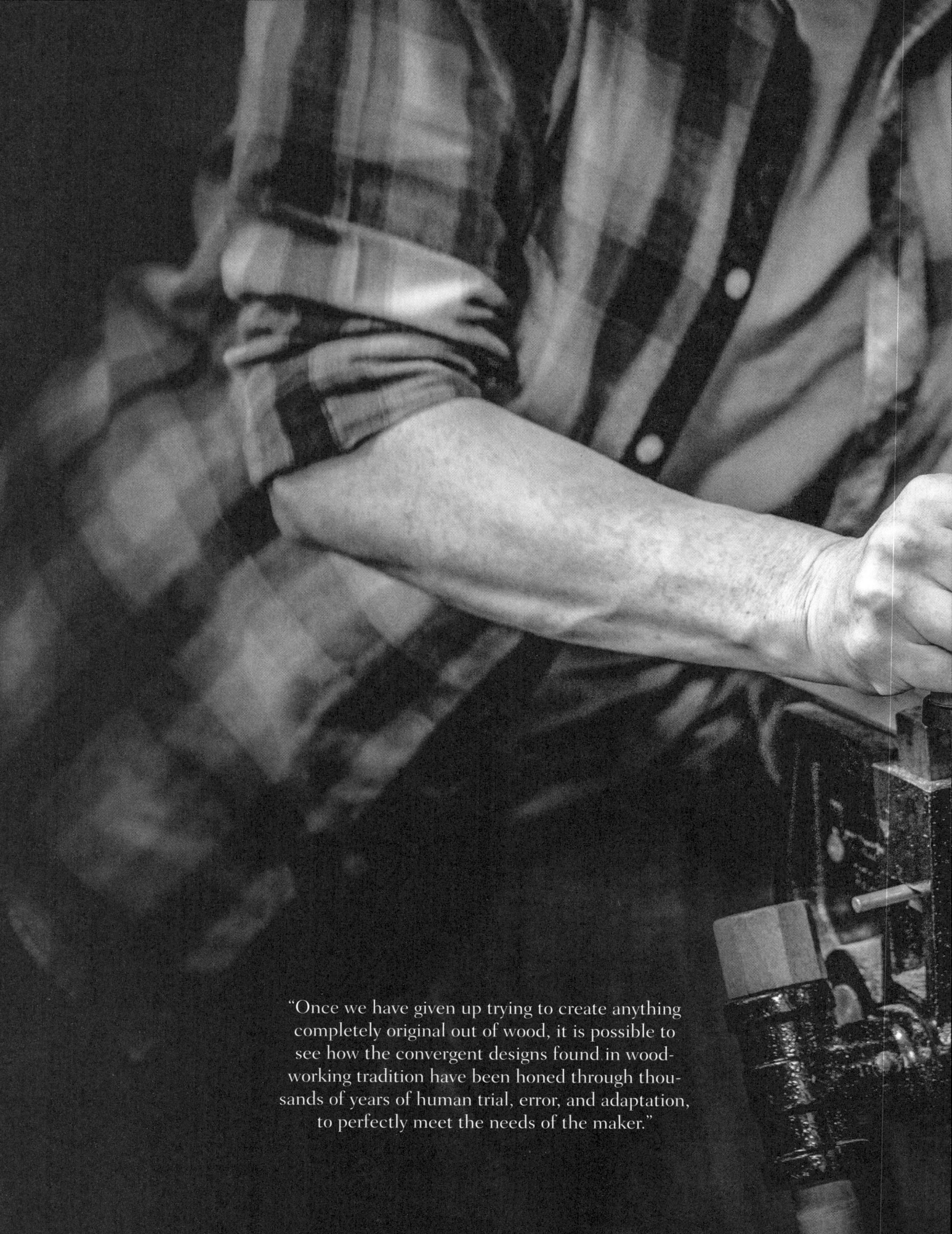

"Once we have given up trying to create anything completely original out of wood, it is possible to see how the convergent designs found in woodworking tradition have been honed through thousands of years of human trial, error, and adaptation, to perfectly meet the needs of the maker."

Photo by Gordon Baer. Courtesy of Kentucky Folk Art Center Archives.

An Unlikely Masterpiece

Examining Chester Cornett's Bookcase Rocking "Chire"

Brendan Bernhardt Gaffney

Photo by Gordon Baer. Courtesy of Kentucky Folk Art Center Archives.

    Chester Cornett was an anachronism in post-World War II Appalachia. While so much of the region had begun its slow introduction to the trends of modern American culture, Cornett lived a close-to-the-ground lifestyle, complete with bare feet, overalls, and a wild mane of hair. When Gurney Norman wrote a lengthy piece in the *Hazard Herald* in 1965 about this largely unknown Appalachian chairmaker titled "Rare Hand-Made Furniture Produced by Bearded Chairmaker," he set off a chain of events that would shape the next two decades of that chairmaker's life.

    Cornett (1913-1981), was a native of the remote Appalachian hollows and hills who spent the better part of his life making all manner of greenwood chairs. In time, Cornett's chairs would become firmly established as remarkable and prized works of art, but what caught the attention of many of those who came to study, photograph, and do business with the rural craftsman were the extremes of both his lifestyle and aesthetic sense. To this day he is remembered as "Hairyman" Cornett (pronounced in the region as "Corn-it"); older inhabitants of Dwarf, Kentucky, recall watching him bring his chairs down from the hill to town on his back.

Even more extreme than his sense of style and way of life were the forms his designs often took – large, bombastic chairs that often had twice the rockers and thrice the carvings of the other chairmakers still working in the backwoods of the mountains. These chairs excited all manner of reaction from the public and his fellow Appalachian craftsmen, from a delight at their novel and whimsical appearance to dismay at their needless complexity or apparent impracticality.

However, despite the renown Cornett received in his lifetime, much of the writing about his life's work focuses on the novelty or extremity of its design and misses his uncompromising abilities as a craftsman. By the middle of the 20th century, many had turned to powered lathes and modern manufacturing techniques, but the bearded Kentuckian was content to keep his hand-powered toolkit. It was with these simple tools that Cornett created a prolific body of work, ranging from simple "settin' chires" that he traded for groceries to the grandiose "two-in-one rockers" that would occasionally bring in several hundred dollars later in his life (and today fetch thousands of dollars at auction).

While many remember or first encounter Cornett as a folk artist whose traumatic life, compulsive drive, and creative energy suit the notions of the "outsider artist," his exploits as a prodigious chairmaker and traditional woodworker do not garner the same attention. A technical study of his work is yet to come, but even a preliminary glance beyond the sometimes unorthodox ornamentation reveals that Cornett worked out these elaborate forms with a solid footing in the Appalachian chairmaking tradition.

This is not to say his abilities as a technician have gone wholly unnoticed. Of the 11 chairs pictured in the introductory chapter of Jennie (née John) Alexander's pivotal book, *Make a Chair From a Tree* (Taunton Press, 1978), three are Cornett's (though they are uncredited). And in Michael Owen Jones' book, *Craftsman of the Cumberlands* (The University Press of Kentucky, 1988), a book that has preserved Cornett's legacy over the decades since his passing, Jones details Cornett's precision and care in his work.

While analyzing Cornett's more complex chairs from a strictly technical viewpoint stands to miss much of the emotion or intent of his creativity, understanding the underlying structure and ability of Cornett serves to highlight the remarkable talent that he employed in making these chairs. For example, examining one of his more ostentatious designs, a rocking chair he called his "two-in-one bookcase rocker, masterpiece of furniture," it's clear that the chair's bold form and ornament stand on a foundation of tradition.

Continued on page 42

Chester Cornett (left) and his family selling dried gourds by the roadside in Dwarf, Kentucky. Photo by Gordon Baer. Courtesy of Kentucky Folk Art Center Archives.

Photo by Taral Thompson. Courtesy of Kentucky Folk Art Center Archives.

A Gallery of Cornett's Work

Original Two-in-One Rocker, early 1960s, walnut and ash.

Mayor's Chair, 1963, walnut and hickory with hickory bark.

Braced Rocker, 1964, white oak and hickory.

Child's Two-in-One Rocker, 1970s, white oak.

Photos by Taral Thompson. Courtesy of Kentucky Folk Art Center Archives.

Snake Chair, 1970s, Honduran mahogany.

Sawed-off Rocker, 1960s-1980, red oak.

Sitting Chair, 1970s, sassafras.

Sitting Chair, 1970s, sassafras.

Cornett in uniform during his deployment in the Aleutian Islands during World War II.
Courtesy of Kentucky Folk Art Center Archives.

A chair made by Cornett's maternal grandfather, Cal Foutch, now in the collection at the Mathers Museum of World Cultures. Note the shape of the slats and the pointed feet, both of which were used and elaborated upon in Cornett's chairs.
Photo by Christopher Schwarz.

Old Kentucky Made

Chester was born in 1913 in Letcher County, Kentucky, to Arthur and Lorraine Cornett. By many accounts, Cornett's early life was unhappy due to both poverty and mistreatment. He attended school sporadically and never advanced past the fourth grade.

Cornett's life did not see any major improvement through his thirties, when he was drafted and deployed to the Aleutian Islands during World War II, an experience that left him traumatized. After more than two years of service, Cornett returned to the mainland, first spending several months in the Ft. George Wright veteran's hospital in Washington state, where he was treated for his trauma. He was eventually sent home to Kentucky on a $50 monthly pension. In his own words, after the war Cornett "could not be satisfied." When he returned home, he sought work in and around Hazard, Kentucky, until he eventually returned to a more rural setting in Dwarf, Kentucky, and went back to the only thing that seemed to set him at ease – making chairs.

If Cornett received any gift as a child, it was learning to make chairs in the traditional manner, a skill passed on by his maternal grandfather, Cal Foutch. Foutch taught the young Cornett traditional skills – how to identify and fell trees for chairs, how to render the logs into usable parts, and how to bend, shape, dry, and refine the parts into the hardy chairs that had been produced in the area for generations.

Chairs would remain Cornett's anchor and calling throughout his life from the age of 16, when he began making them for sale. Living on only his disability pension from the military, Cornett spent the majority of his adult life trying to augment that income practicing his trade. And while he certainly lived to make chairs, it rarely provided significant earnings. He made a number of attempts to alter or improve on the traditional designs as a means of generating income, going so far as to make a run of 50 folding chairs for a traveling movie theater for $1 each and making bar stools for the local town watering hole.

While Cornett toiled, his creative compulsion expanded beyond these classic forms in the 1950s to those for which he came to be known later in life. It may be impossible to understand the exact reasons and creative inspirations that Cornett drew on when he created his more lavish forms which often included elaborately carved homilies and dedications, oversized finials, luxuriously woven seats, baskets, backrests, hidden storage, or footrests – but there are several plausible explanations.

For one, Cornett was repeatedly rewarded by his customers for his novel designs. While he fetched no more than $20 for his standard rocking chairs, and half that for his plain post-and-rung chairs, by 1965 (the year Norman

Cornett's workshop. Photo by Chester Cornett. Courtesy of Kentucky Folk Art Center Archives.

wrote about him in the *Hazard Herald*) Cornett was selling the "two-in-one" style rockers for up to $100. It's worth noting, however, that he reported these chairs to take between 300 and 500 hours to make. In fact, it was the small chairs and rockers he produced, along with simple dried gourds and other crafts such as baskets, that accounted for the majority of Cornett's $865 income in 1965 (roughly $7,000 today, adjusted for inflation). He may have considered the larger chairs a means of making a more premium product, though he also seemed to believe that they may have been more work than he could afford to invest in a single chair.

A more likely reason for the growing complexity of Cornett's chairs came from his romantic vision of older forms, which he expressed in his opinion of his own work. Cornett talked frequently of "Old Kentucky," a time and place he sought out and seemed to believe was his true home. And his throne-like chairs, with their near-Gothic appearances and decorative motifs, seem to recall an older, royal aesthetic. In Jones' book, Cornett speculates that his work was "too early, or some'n or other, or too late." Jones, as a scholar of folk crafts, elaborates on this point, imagining the chairs as "generating a feeling of power or control as well as a sense of protective seclusion."

Whatever the reasons are for Cornett's novel designs, Jones notes that, in spite of his whimsical design tendencies, Cornett was "certainly a master craftsman." While it is tempting to take in the full body of the chairmaker's work to evaluate that claim, I believe we can find all the detail, technical ability, and mastery of craft in a single piece – one Cornett would come to call his masterpiece.

A page from Cornett's ledger, showing his income for October and November of 1965. Note that two chairs sold for $33.90, but the majority of the sales were gourds and potatoes; there is even an entry for a tool repair, 'handled an ax,' for $2.50. Courtesy of Kentucky Folk Art Center Archives.

Photo by Christopher Schwarz.

Two-in-one Bookcase Rocker, Masterpiece of Furniture

When I began reading about Cornett, one piece jumped out of his prolific body of work as powerful, odd, and novel – a chair Jones refers to in his book as "the Masterpiece." The chair, with its shelves, four rockers, pinned oak panels, and walnut ornamentation, was a work that puzzled even its creator.

"This one is Made so different that hit don't look like iney chair that I Ever made. They are somtin strange about this Rockin chire I don't Reley no what hapin I just started working on hit Seems to Be sometime Kidin me so strang," Cornett wrote in a letter to Jones, who would eventually be presented with the special rocker in place of the seven-slat rocker he'd ordered. Cornett was driven to create the chair by some unusual force, and to it he added ornament and parts for more than a month, saying "Sem to Be sumtin new about Ever day has got to Be Adied   Hit is so hevey now that I can't hardly lift hit." As Jones notes, "Chester was by nature planful in his work." Yet this particular chair seemed to push back against Cornett's usually deliberate chairmaking practice, driving him to create a novel piece of furniture.

Upon inspection of the chair, which now resides in the archives of the Mathers Museum of World Cultures in Bloomington, Indiana, it is clear that whatever brought Cornett to make such an elaborate form did nothing to attenuate its creator's care and skill in construction. The chair's basic frame resembles that of his other "two-in-one" rockers, with eight posts serving as eight legs, between which a number of rungs span to create the structure, and four long sawn rockers below provide the smooth footing. It also features Cornett's signature octagonal finials, which sit atop each post; each rung's intersection with a post is pinned with small carved pins, another feature Cornett saw as a sort of calling card for his "Old Kentucky" style of construction.

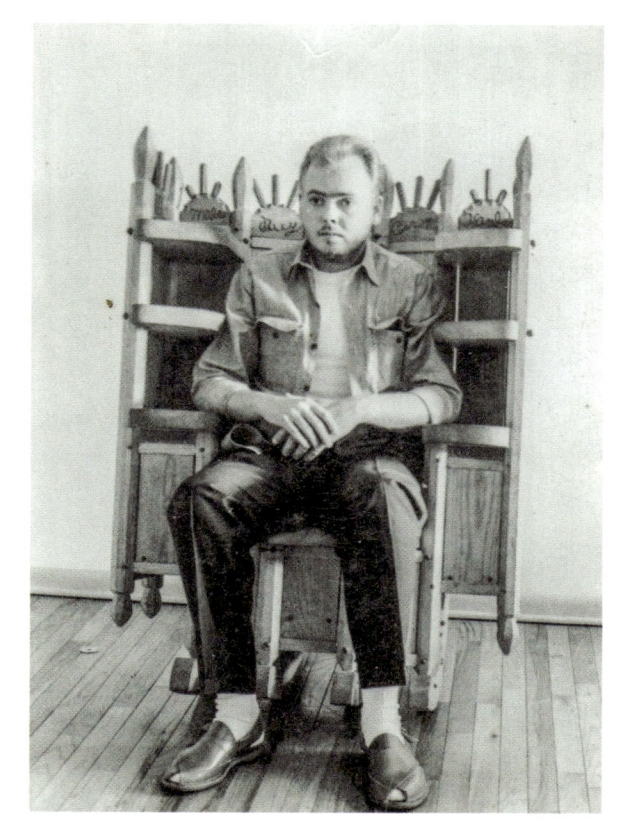

Michael Owen Jones, Cornett's biographer, sits in the bookcase rocker for a photo. Jones would be given the rocker in place of the seven-slat rocking chair he ordered.
Photo by Chester Cornett. Courtesy of Kentucky Folk Art Center Archives.

However, it is at that point that Cornett went a different direction with this particular creation. Where he would normally leave the space between posts and rungs empty (save for the slats behind the sitter), on this chair each negative space is fitted with an oak panel, which is captured above and below in grooves in the adjacent rungs. Cornett also made four additional posts, two on each side, which are attached with the rung-and-panel construction – this addition allows for the extension of the armrest into a series of shelves above, and a storage space below, the armrest. And, continuing the trend of filling in space which would normally be left empty, Cornett fit a series of scalloped half-circle ornaments and small carved pins between the top of each of the eight tall posts, in a motif reminiscent of a rising sun. Onto these ornaments he carved an inscription with a Buck knife, which reads, "Old Kentucky Made Buy Chester Cornett's Hands Engle Mill." (Engle Mill is the locality outside of Dwarf, Kentucky where Cornett's shop and home were located.)

While it is interesting to address how Cornett's form departed from its normal road so much in this piece, it is even more rewarding to consider how such a complex construction would have been fabricated. To better understand just how masterfully the chair is constructed, it is worth examining the complexities introduced by the addition of each new detail, and how those eccentricities pushed Cornett's abilities to an incredible degree of precision and care.

Making a Masterpiece

It can be assumed that Cornett knew the bookcase rocker would be complex. The decision to fill the normally empty space between the posts with captured panels must have been made early on – each rung needed a groove (in Cornett's case, most likely chiseled) into one side before the parts were fit in the first steps of assembly. The panels must also have been present at the first stages of building the chair, which means that the dimensions of most of the chair, and the spatial relationships of each piece, must have been locked in before any assembly could take place – a decision that is not normally required at the outset of making one of Cornett's standard chairs.

It is also worth noting that only the posts, rockers, and rungs appear to have been constructed using split green wood – the armrests, shelves, panels, and seat all bear marks of a powered planer, a machine Cornett never owned. Cornett occasionally went to lumberyards to purchase dried wood for his more elaborate chairs, as his process of dimensioning wood by hand was, he supposed, inefficient in rendering thick, flat stock.

However, Cornett's use of store-bought lumber did not compromise his traditional greenwood joinery techniques. Because the posts, rungs, and rockers were all from split green wood, he could bend, rive, and selectively dry the tenons of the parts in the traditional manner, allowing for the hardy joinery that makes a greenwood chair so strong. Furthermore, the joinery used on the chair is even more complex than his standard style of round tenons, incorporating rectangular pinned tenons at the bottom of each post where it is joined with the rocker, a detail that would have provided more support and reinforcement for the added weight of the chair.

Rather than using standard round tenons to join the posts to the rockers, Cornett used pinned rectangular tenons and mortises, lending more strength to what Cornett must have realized was going to be a heavy chair.

It is fortuitous that Cornett stuck with the strong joinery. Judging by his words about the continual additions and how certain parts were attached, it appears he added the thick shelves, hinged armrests, and ornaments after the chair's initial assembly, which added significant weight. The shelves are pinned to the panels and posts in a manner that would've allowed their fitting and assembly later in the process of construction, and that enabled Cornett to carve details into each.

First, the middle shelf on each side of the chair was relieved to allow the sitter's upper arms and shoulders room when the armrests were used. This detail becomes essential when one realizes just how cocoon-like the chair is, with hardly enough room between the shelves for most shoulder spans. The corner of each shelf was also scribed and cut to let in the posts at each corner, which project past the panels.

The armrests themselves are shaped and relieved like the other shelves above, with the addition of hinges that allow access to the enclosed space below. Cornett made several chairs that incorporated some form of storage below the armrests or seat, which he referred to as "baskets." In order to incorporate this convenience on the bookcase rocker, he had to contend with a number of added problems. For one, the hinged armrests needed to be mortised into, to allow the top of the post to sit inside the bottom of the armrest (shown on 48, top right); cutting the top of the post any shorter would have weakened the topmost rung's joinery.

The top rungs below the front of the armrest are also modified, built up by an additional piece of oak. This brought them level with their adjacent rungs and supported the armrest both down its length and across its width (shown on 48, top left). This added piece is necessary because of how

The eccentric armrests were incorporated into the design with a number of additions and complications. Each thick armrest is relieved where the post projects into its underside, and the top rungs of the front panels have a second piece of wood added (engraved with "book" and "case" on the front sides) to support the armrest at the front and side when closed.

Cornett offset the tenons of each rung when joined to the post; to allow for a deeper mortise, and therefore stronger joinery, each rung on the chair is staggered in height relative to its adjacent rungs. This staggered construction added strength and a technical hurdle; each panel had to be fashioned individually. It is clear that Cornett was improvising when he built this piece. But thanks to his skilled mind and hands, it feels no less solid or deliberate than one built from detailed plans.

  The sum of these details spell out a clear narrative; that Cornett, while certainly egged on by wildly creative compulsions, was no less a technician and master of his tools than those furniture makers who find their work exhibited as fine art, not "outsider art." While the aesthetic and novelty of his work voice troubled thoughts and a desire for rosier times, Cornett's work speaks to dextrous, stable hands and a mind untroubled by its ignorance of writing, instead satisfied by a mastery of rendering its imaginative ideas in solid wood. ◆

Cornett pinned every joint on the chair with wooden pegs, some of which are carefully carved in a fluted design. Here, the middle shelf is pinned to both the front post and the side panel, and the rung's tenon into the post is pinned as well. There are more than 100 pegs on this chair, all of which were hewn by hand from hickory using a hatchet and knife.

Photographer unknown. Courtesy of Kentucky Folk Art Center Archives.

"They are somtin strange about this Rockin chire   I don't Reley no what hapin   I just started working on hit Seems to Be sometime Kidin me   so strang,"

– Chester Cornett

Coopering: A Harsh Mistress

Marshall Scheetz

A simple wooden cask can tell the story of an extraordinary trade. This mundane container was used to ship valuable and extravagant products such as gunpowder, wine, whale oil, sugar, rum, glass, and ceramics. It may surprise some that while the contents have been much studied, the containers and the cooper's trade have been studied hardly at all. The mystique of the trade is confounded by the simple form: a conical cylinder comprised of wooden slats held fast by rings. The trade and its products are unassuming, utilitarian, but ubiquitous. Casks and buckets were part of the historical landscape, used for shipping virtually everything and used in every home for storage and domestic chores.

A wooden bucket has been a necessity for ages. Nearly everyone hauled water from source to home or work. Cooperage requires regular use – it is vulnerable to moisture changes over time, and if allowed to dry out, may fall apart. Most cooperage doesn't survive because, when the vessel inevitably wore out, it was cast aside as useless.

The trade of the cooper is divided into wet (tight), dry (slack), and white coopering. The tight cooper makes barrels for receiving a variety of different liquids: beer, wine, oil, vinegar, water, and spirits. A dry or slack cooper makes casks used to contain dry goods: powders, sugar, linens, biscuits, grain, and nails. A white cooper makes an assortment of domestic containers used for chores in the home or on the farm: buckets, tubs, tankards, and churns; straight-sided containers which still possess a conical form. The term "bouge work" identifies cooperage with a belly or a bouge: barrels and casks.

In every industry there were specific styles of coopering. While one cooper may only have produced casks for the brewing industry, another may have served his time at sea on a whaling ship, making, repairing, and maintaining casks for oil. Grist mills employed specialized coopers to make flour barrels. Gunpowder mills needed powder kegs bound in saplings or copper to avoid sparks. A dry/slack cooper versed in flour barrels or nail kegs wasn't expected to make stout liquid-tight pipes, puncheons, tuns, or hogsheads, and a brewer's cooper, or another tight/wet cooper, couldn't possibly keep pace with someone knocking out six flour barrels a day.[1] It is difficult to overestimate the importance of coopers to period industries. "About the most important single article of equipment aboard a whaler was the cask, and one of the most important men on shipboard and one who always commanded a good lay (share) was the cooper."[2]

In my early 20s, I had the life-changing opportunity to serve a traditional apprenticeship under master cooper James Pettengell. Mr. Pettengell came from a family of coopers in London, England, and served his time as an apprentice making beer casks at Whitbread's Brewery. James and his brother George set up shop at Colonial Williamsburg in the early 1970s, producing barrels and buckets using hand tools as they had been taught as apprentices a generation earlier. At Colonial Williamsburg, I saw a unique opportunity to learn from a tradition unbroken since the 18th century. Preservation of trade knowledge and putting that knowledge into practice turned out to be my *raison d'être*. After a six-year apprenticeship, I worked as a journeyman under Mr. Pettengell at the Colonial Williamsburg Foundation from 2008 to 2015.

When I started on my journey as a cooper, I had no serious previous woodworking experience. In some ways, this may have helped me work through the apprenticeship. In the beginning, I can recall, without exception, that every tool I picked up for the first time felt awkward and unnatural, from the canted handle of the axe to the seemingly excessive weight of the hammer and drawknives. Cooper's tools tend to be bulky and heavy, especially for brewers/wine/spirits work. I remember thinking that these tools looked like they came straight out of a medieval torture chamber.

I was initially drawn into this trade because of its rich history. I love pulling together the insights from my apprenticeship and discovering the parallels with primary and archaeological records. Studying old barrels and buckets is wonderful because it is a vivid sensory experience: oily residue left on 19th-century whaling barrels; antebellum molasses oozing out of barrel staves excavated from the Missouri River; Revolutionary War tar buckets staining notes and fingers; the pungent vinegar smell of old cider casks. Curators at museums, historical institutes, and national parks are helpful when approached with a keen interest in their collections. Very often they aren't completely aware of all the amazing cooperage they possess; it's overlooked for more elegant artifacts such as furniture or iron work.

"Coopering is a harsh mistress," my master would always say. If you step away from the trade for any length of time, it takes a while to "get your hand back into it." Coopering exacts a physical toll on its practitioners as well. A 19th-century London sociologist wrote, "Coopers become prematurely old, suffering greatly from pains in the chest, and across the back, attributable to their bending over their hot work. A cooper at large work is an old man, sir, at forty…his physical energies then are nearly exhausted."[3] But at the same time, Mr. Pettengell often compares the act of coopering to an elegant dance. Producing stout oak casks requires brute strength, but also a dancer's grace, efficient movements, and exacting tolerances to produce a liquid-tight vessel.

As with any apprenticeship of a skilled trade, over years of practice the body grows into the work and the use of the specific tools of the job. The fatigue of the apprentice's arm in the first year eventually wanes as muscle, ligament, and tendon strengthen. More efficient positions and leverage points are learned through practice, and by watching those more skilled in the trade.

Mechanical Processes of Traditional Coopering

There is a distinct lack of historical treatises on the rules and practices of coopers. Anyone looking for an 18th-century instruction manual on making barrels will be disappointed. There is, however, a tremendous amount of information about coopering tightly woven into industrial business records. Casks were strictly regulated shipping containers both for consumer protection and tax purposes. Read through the dusty statutes of the American British colonies, and you'll uncover exacting requirements for coopers to follow. Failure to achieve proper cask labels and size put a cooper at risk of severe fines and damaged reputation.[4]

The instructions below are in no way meant to replace the experiences and lessons learned from a full six-year apprenticeship in coopering. I hope, rather, that they offer some insight into what seems to be a mysterious set of skills. Most of the work involved in coopering is measured by eye and feel. Although there are few absolute measuring tools involved in the trade, you will find there are boundaries in which a cooper's work is confined and regulated, as will be described below.

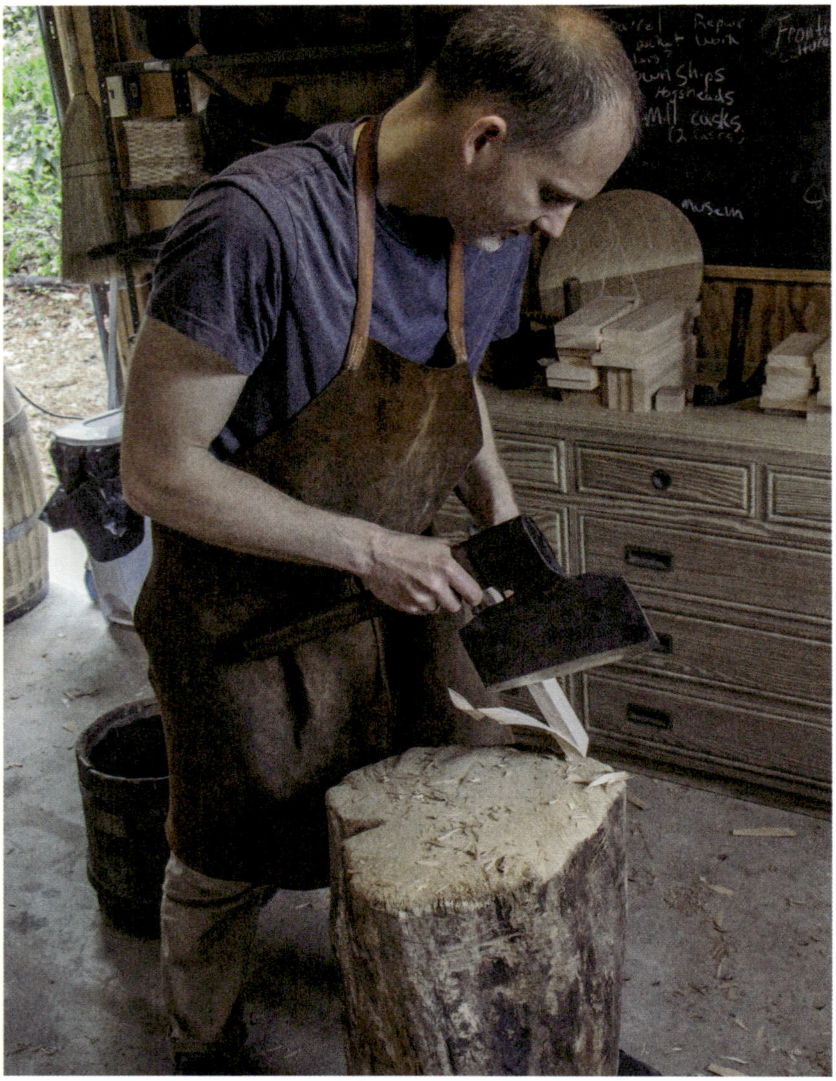
Repair
Work
Hogsheads
Museum

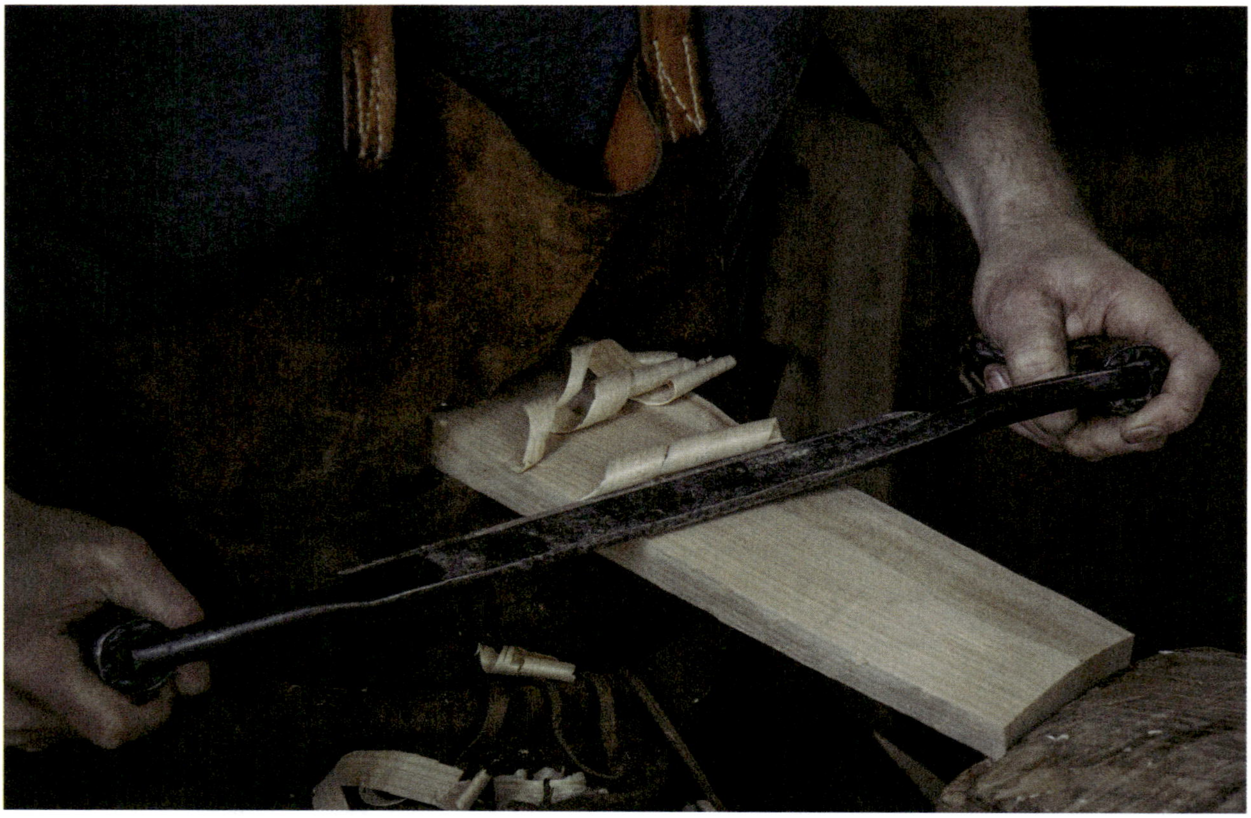

Acquiring Proper Stock

Traditional coopering in Europe employed quarter-split or riven wood to make the walls and heads of the vessels. In a world where sawing was time-consuming, splitting straight-grained logs into flat bolts of wood was the most expeditious processing method. Riving a knot-free log is a satisfying experience, because it's surprising how easily it yields to iron wedges, wooden gluts, and a froe.

Quarter-split material is a pleasure to work with hands tools, even after several years of seasoning. Any type of wood that grows with clear grain, quartered from a mature log, is ideal for coopering. Different species historically used for coopering include red and white oak, chestnut, white ash, spruce, fir, yellow pine, white pine, tulip poplar, cypress, and white cedar. Examples never used in industry because of their irregular grain include walnut, elm, maple, hickory, and fruit wood.

Quarter-split white oak is always my preferred wood of choice, but time constraints force me to use quartersawn white oak on many projects. Clear, straight grained, face-sawn cypress and white cedar are what I have available for many smaller bits of cooperage.

The stock should be a consistent thickness throughout. The width of the stave material may vary, but a consistent width does aid in the shaping and fitting process. Thickness of stock may vary depending on the size of the container and product being held. The same species of wood is used throughout a single container to avoid differing expansion and contraction rates.

Cooperage Practice

A cooper's berth (workspace) was comprised of a chopping block, drawbench or shaving horse (if needed), tool chest, bick iron (cooper's anvil), and kit of cooper's tools. Historically, nobody enters your berth except you.

The shape of a coopered vessel is defined by hoops. They are the closest thing to a template a cooper uses, and they act as scaffolding to erect the container. Called truss hoops, ring hoops, or raising hoops, they are vital tools for even the most basic cooperage. These hoops should be perfectly round and flared to match the conical shape of the desired vessel. They are made of thick, sturdy wood or iron because they must sustain abuse from repeated use, and this rigidity helps them maintain their shape. Coopers working jointly with specific industries possess sets of truss hoops for each standard-sized cask: flour barrels, tobacco hogsheads, sugar hogsheads, etc. The brewing industry demanded numerous sizes: firkins, 9 gallons; kilderkins, 18 gallons; barrels, 36 gallons; tierces, 42 gallons; hogsheads, 54 gallons; puncheons, 84 gallons. Gunpowder, too, was stored in standard-size casks: barrel, 100 pounds; half-barrel, 50 pounds; keg (quarter-barrel), 25 pounds; half-keg, 12-1/2 pounds; quarter-keg, 6-1/4 pounds. Each size cask required a separate set of truss hoops, used each time a cask of that size was built. The quality of the work and efficiency of production grow exponentially on a run of a certain size. The importance of using a quality set of hoops to make standard-sized containers over and over cannot be overemphasized. Repetition trains the eye to see the needed curvature and angles.

Listing the Staves

The primary workstation of a cooper is the chopping block. The initial shaping of staves and heads begins with the cooper's side axe at the block. "Take your foot off that block," my master told me once before he explained that the dirt from the bottom of shoes finds its way into the wood. Dirt embedded in the block is an abrasive, dulling your axe every time you sink it into the block.

The axe is used to remove large amounts of wood, revealing the tapered shape of each stave and the beveled edges where the staves will meet inside the hoops. The more work done with an axe at the block, the less work is required with finer tools. Neat work done with the axe also slows the wear on the rest of your tools.

Listing (tapering the staves) is often a practice of bouge-work coopers working with harder woods, such as oak. An axe isn't a necessity when working softer woods such as cedar or white pine. Drawknives and jointer planes are excellent (and safer) substitutes for the axe on these woods.

Backing the Staves

The backing knife is a standard flat drawknife used to cut the convex curvature on the back (outside) of the staves. The knife is rocked across the surface, slicing away more from the edges of the stave and little or nothing from the middle. At this stage it's easiest to keep the raising hoops nearby and repeatedly hold the stave inside the hoop to reference the curvature needed. Once the curvature is cut at the narrow end of the stave, it is carried through to the opposing end. A novice may find it helpful to hold the other end of the stave up against the larger hoops in the set.

As staves are shaped, they are held in place using one of two different methods. Coopers making casks do most of the shaping at the chopping block, wedging the staves between themselves and block hooks attached to the chopping block. This method, while expedient, is inconvenient for shaping staves for shorter vessels such as buckets, kegs, and wash tubs.

White coopers usually use a drawbench to secure staves for backing and hollowing. I was trained on a drawbench quite similar to a 19th-century "cooper's mare" in the collections at the Mariners' Museum in Newport News, Virginia.

Cooper's Drawbench in the collections of The Mariners' Museum, Newport News, Virginia, Accession Number 1934.0642.000001

Hollowing the Staves

Hollowing knives possess a curvature for carving out a radius to match that of different-sized containers. The curvature of the hollowing knife does not need to be an exact match to the container, as its radius allows for a range of similar sizes. The curvature of the inside of the stave is cut to match the exterior curvature previously cut with the backing knife. Many hollowing knives found in the antique market have a shallow curvature, designed for hollowing barrel staves, not bucket staves.

Jointing the Staves

The cooper's long jointer is a finishing tool used for cutting the flat butt joint where two staves meet inside a hoop. As previously noted, the surface to be cut is first roughed out with the axe, creating less work to be done with the jointer. The sole of the plane is dead flat, and the iron is straight. Years of practice allow the cooper to hold the stave at the correct angle to make repeated passes across the blade until a well-fitting butt joint is achieved at the correct angle for the corresponding container.

In the modern woodworking world, there seems to be a dependence on measuring devices and tools that cut an exact shape, angle, or curvature on a piece of wood. But traditional coopering is a sensory-intense trade. While jointing staves, the craftsperson learns to judge the angle by eye, and the fingers develop a sensitivity for imperfections that would prevent two surfaces from closing to make a watertight fit. Additionally, listening to how much material is being sliced off with each pass is just as important as running a finger across the freshly cut surface.

Accurate jointing is a difficult skill mastered through years of repetition. The best way to practice is to shape one piece after another, fitting stave to stave inside the raising hoop.

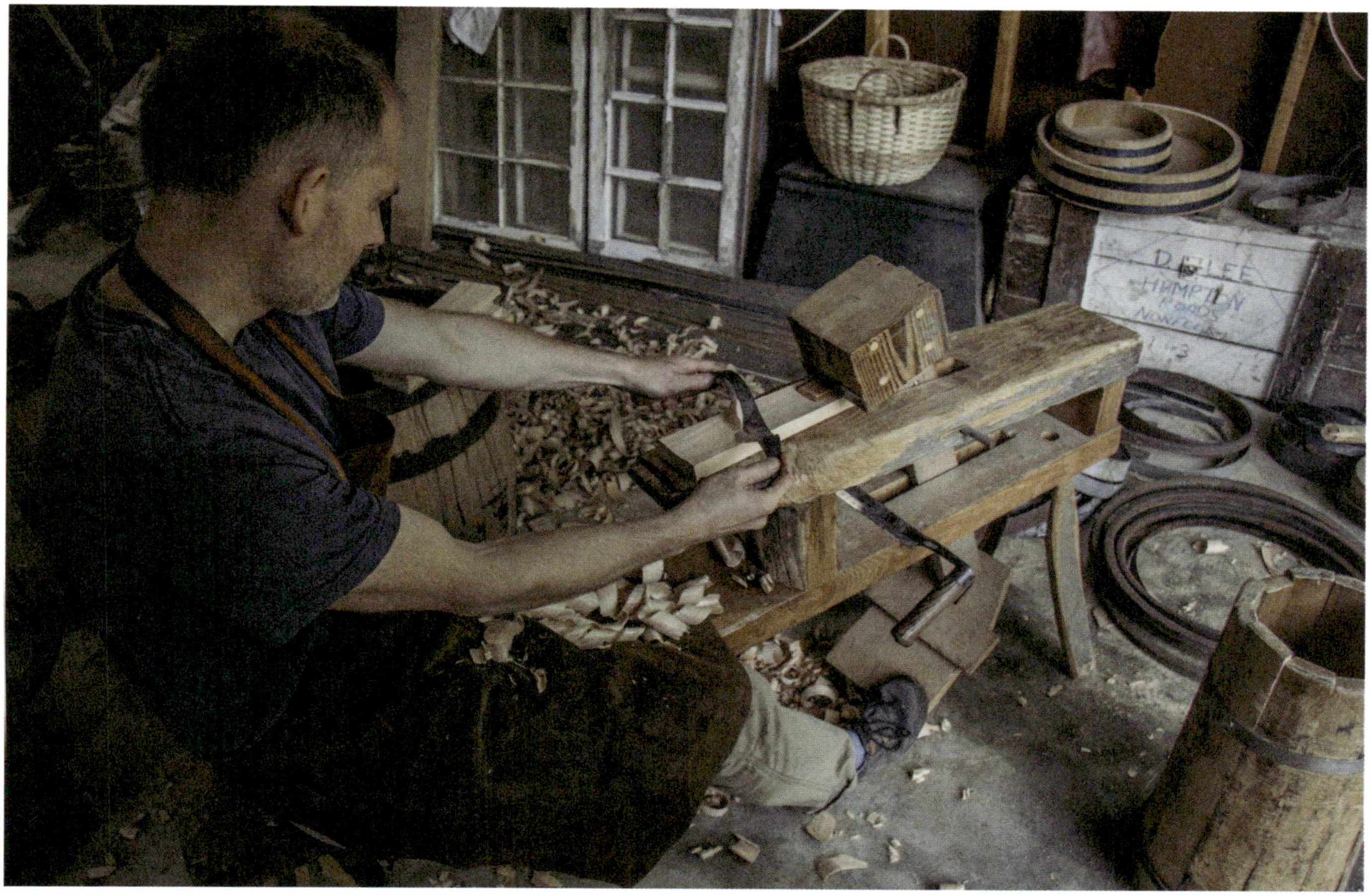
HAMPTON
ROADS

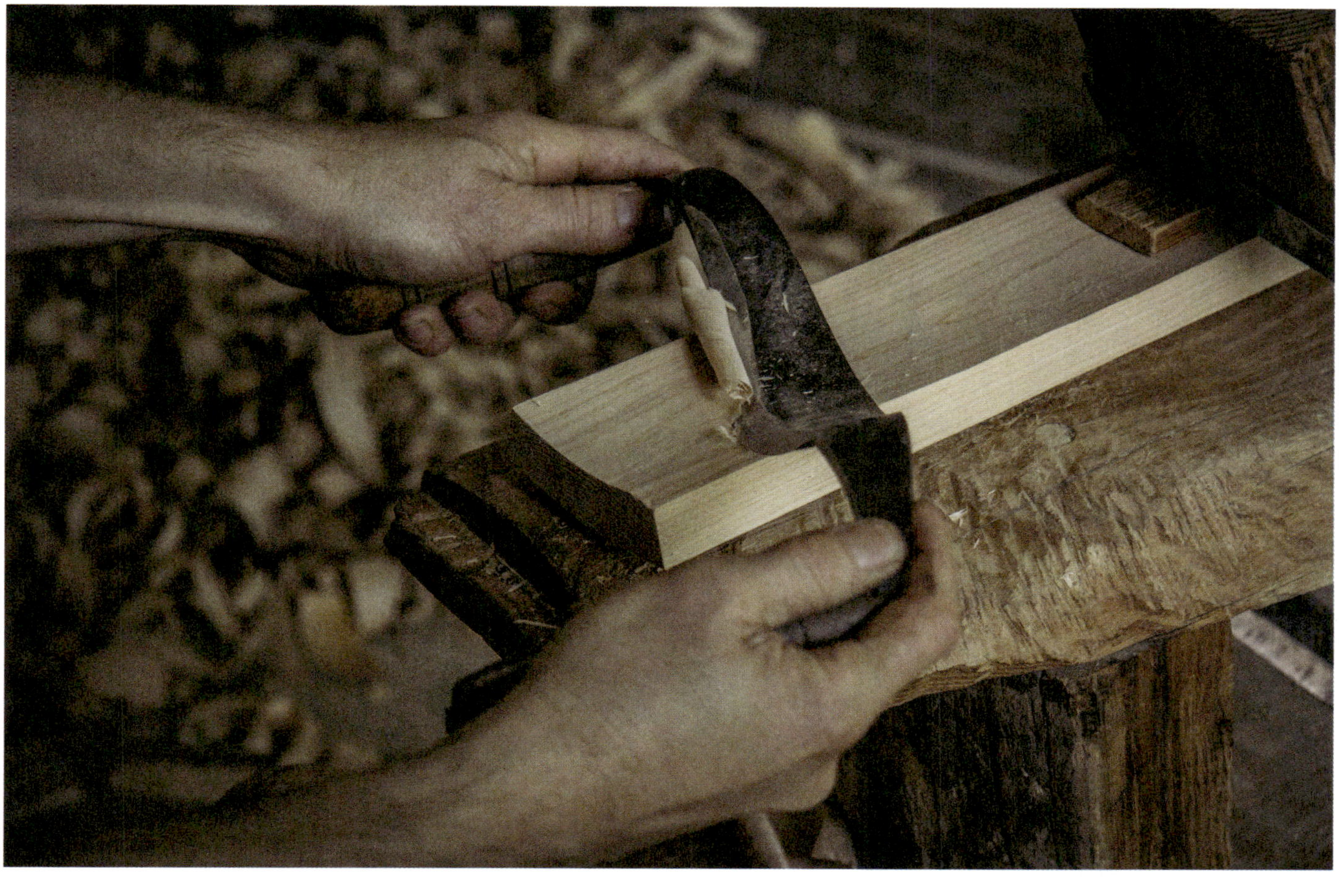

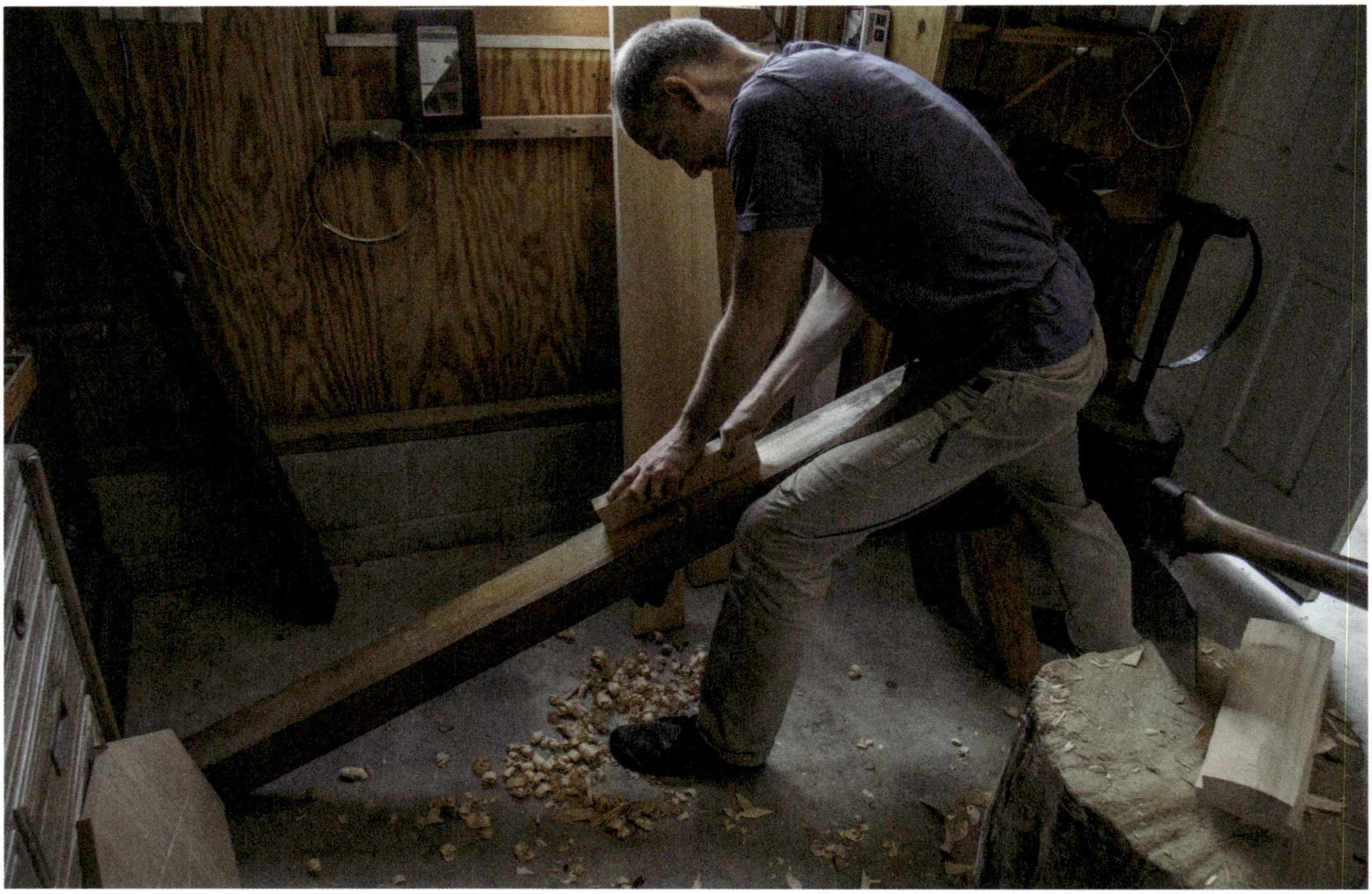

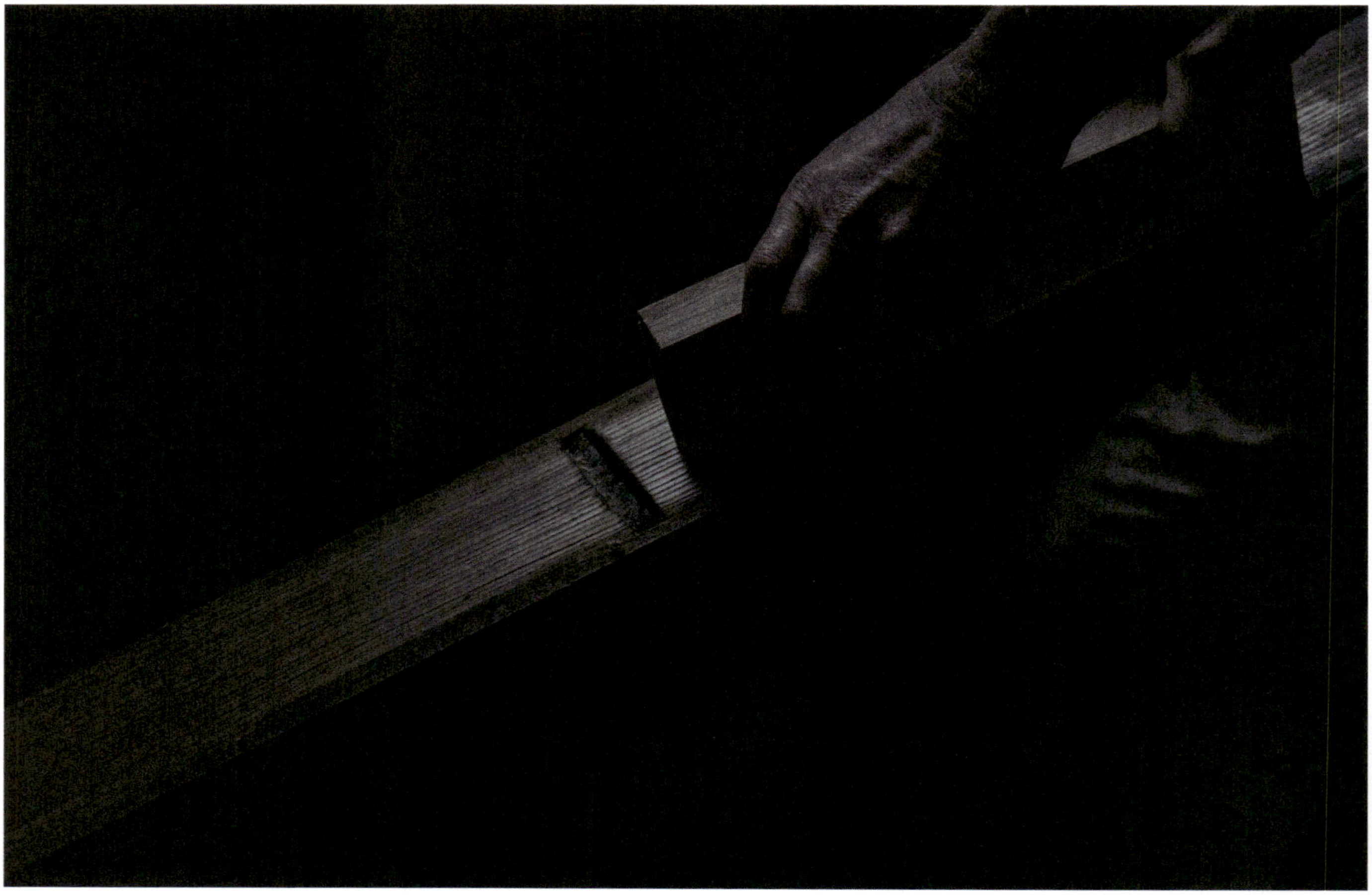

Raising Up

Once all the staves have been listed, backed, hollowed, and jointed, it's time to raise them up into the hoops. The easiest way to raise up a bucket is to stack the staves, narrow end up, into the smallest raising hoop. This prevents the rings from sliding down off the container after raising, and it also makes it easy to remove and modify each stave if a joint is not tight. Clamping the staves against the raising hoop with bent pieces of hoop iron is one way to keep the staves from falling inward before the hoop is filled. Once assembled, the raising hoop should rest slightly above the top of the staves. After all the hoops are hammered tight, the raising hoop should be seated about 1/2" below the end of the staves.

  At this stage, it is possible to see if the joints are closed. Joints that are open on the exterior are referred to as "hard joints," while those open on the interior are called "soft joints." Both are unacceptable in wet cooperage, so incorrectly fit staves should be removed, rejointed, and placed back inside the hoop. This is done until all the joints close easily even before tightening the hoops. If there are ridges and discrepancies from the back of one stave to another, the stave with the elevated surface will encounter greater pressure from the hoops. This, in turn, will push the cask out of round, distorting the shape over time and weakening the cask. Material is removed with each correction, reducing the width of the stave. Many corrections may remove too much material, allowing the raising hoop to slide down lower than it should. Narrow staves may need to be replaced with wider staves. The raising hoop needs to be filled to ensure proper volume of the container.

Trussing: Firing the Barrel & Driving the Hoops

Coopering demands seasoned wood. Green lumber, while flexible and easy to shape, shrinks over time, allowing hoops to loosen and resulting in the eventual collapse of the vessel. Moisture in green wood would be released into the interior of the cask, causing spoilage of its contents. Dried timber, while far less flexible than green timber, can be bent by applying heat. While many woodworkers employ moisture as a conduit to transfer heat into wood, traditional coopers use dry heat for bouge-work. Bystanders are often startled to see open flame inside a barrel under construction, but used in this way, fire is a tool just like any other in the cooper's tool box. It is not a destructive force; rather, the cooper harnesses this element to coax the wood into a new form. He asks it to bend; he cajoles it.

Shavings and chips left over from shaping the staves are used to create a small, controlled fire inside a metal cage called a cresset, which is placed inside the cask. The intent of the firing is to warm the staves, not char or toast them. Over a period of 15-20 minutes, the cooper uses the uncalloused back of his hand to check the warmth of the exterior of the staves. Experience tells the cooper when it's time to start driving the hoops down. A series of different-sized truss hoops are driven from the middle of the cask to the ground. Once the bottom of the cask is the same diameter as the middle, it's flipped over and smaller hoops are driven onto the opposing end to further close the joints. Usually, it takes between four and 10 hoops to completely truss a cask.

Pompeiing

After the cask is bent, the second heating, known as "pompeiing," is required to harden the staves to their new shape. At this point, there remains a great deal of spring tension in the bend of the staves. A hotter, second firing stabilizes the cask and relaxes the lignum in the wood. A loose lid is placed over the cask to help control the fire by depriving it of oxygen and also traps heat inside. Later when the hoops are removed to install the heads, there will be very little spring/opening to the staves. No charring is necessary, but some refer to this stage as "toasting."

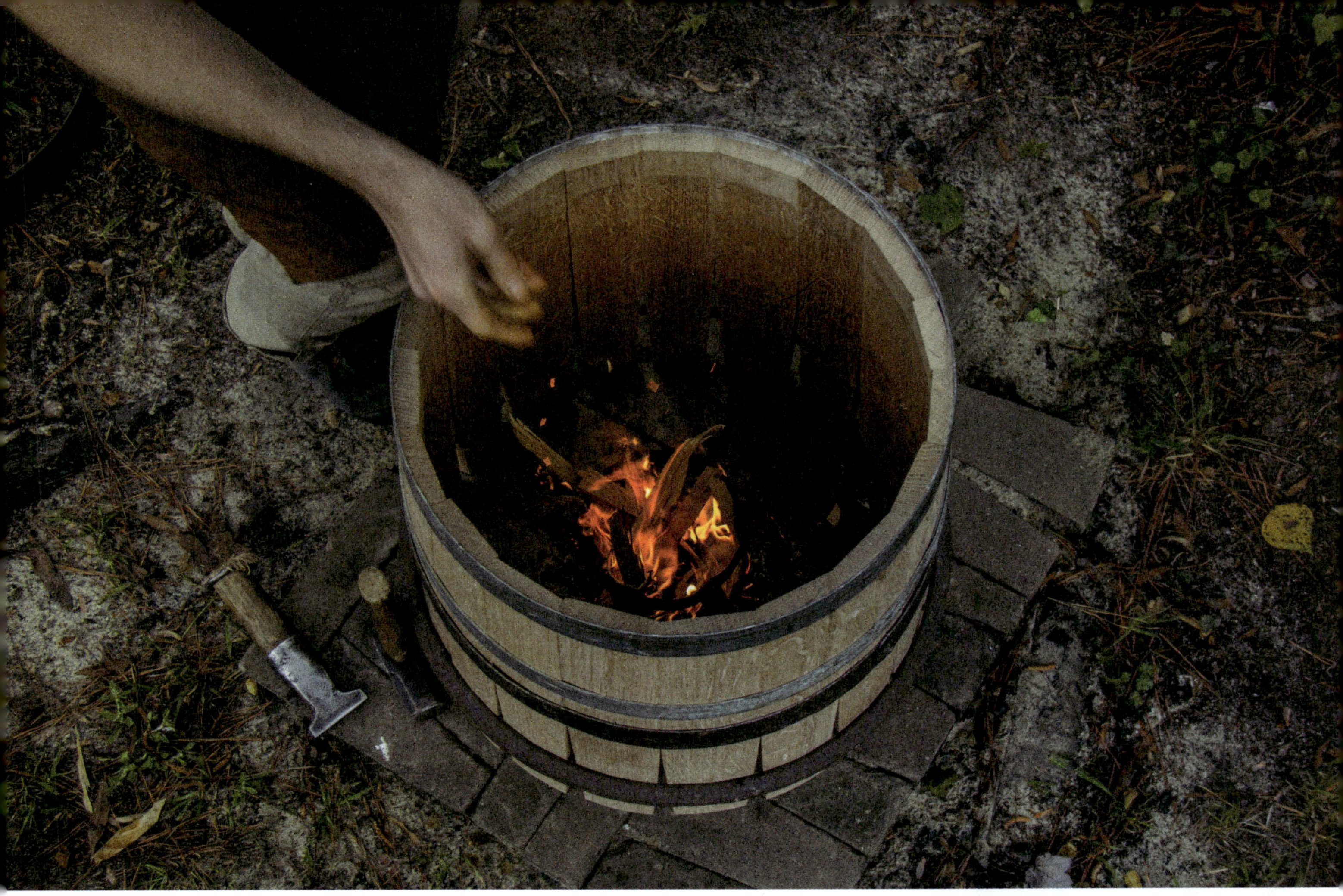

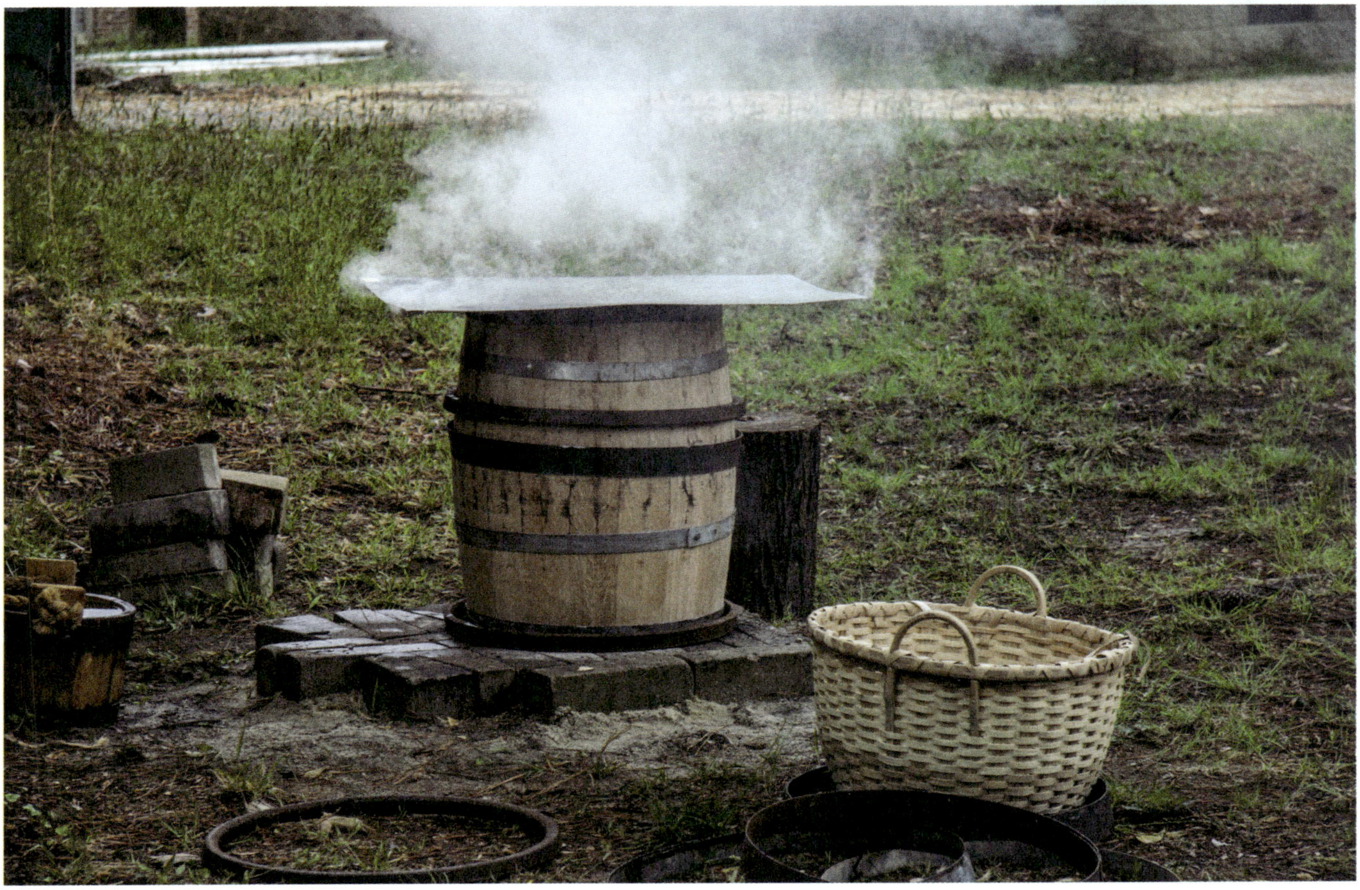

Rounding Off

While a barrel is probably one of the strongest wooden objects produced by humans, it is not indestructible. The most vulnerable part of the barrel is the "chime," the ends of the staves beyond the heads. There are many subtle steps a cooper performs to help protect and strengthen this weak link in an otherwise sturdy vessel. Once the cask is trussed up and fired, it should be rounded off, chived, crozed, headed up, and hooped, all before the staves cool.

Rounding off (chamfering the ends of the staves) is done with a cooper's adze. The ends of the staves are chopped with a chamfer running down to the interior of the cask, leaving the outside edge of the stave untouched for now. This serves two purposes – first, by chamfering the edges of the staves toward the inside of the barrel, this surface is protected from ground contact and possible chipping or breakage into the groove that holds the head. Secondly, the thin outer edge of the chime makes it easy to level with the sun plane. An adze is used when working with dense woods such as oak or ash, while a drawknife is generally sufficient for working softer woods such as cedar, cypress, or pine.

A sun plane or topping plane is essentially a curved jack plane, radiused to accommodate the circular shape of the container. It's important to keep the plane from rocking as it's pushed across the top of the barrel. Little effort is needed to level the thin outer edge of the staves.

Once the staves are level, there are a few different tools that can be used to smooth the interior surface of the cask where the groove will be cut. A crumming knife (or jigger) is a type of drawknife that works well on larger casks. A chiv (or howell) is a type of plane with a table that rests on the ends of the staves. It slides around the top of the cask, cutting across the grain. A scorp is a tool that may be used on softer woods to ensure the interior surface is consistent. If this surface is not level, the depth of the groove will vary, preventing a proper fit of the head. This juncture of the head to the staves is one of the most critical fits in coopering.

Crozing

"Croze" is the name of both the groove in the cask that holds a head in place, and the tool that cuts it. The tool is placed on the top of the bucket or barrel, held tight, and swung around the inside until the groove is cut. Finding a way to properly secure the barrel or bucket while crozing can be a challenge. Overall, the croze is a temperamental tool and difficult to master.

There are several different types of crozes. Evidence shows the earliest type of croze in the trade is the saw tooth croze. The hawksbill croze, which seems to have come into use in the 19th century, cuts a superior (crisp, clean, square) groove but tends to be more difficult to set up than the others. A V-notch groove was historically used for slack work, or dry cooperage like potato barrels, apple barrels, etc., although it is sometimes used in tight work nowadays.

Saw Tooth Croze

Hawksbill Croze

Fitting Heads

Technically speaking, barrels do not have tops and bottoms – they have two heads. Heads and staves are always made from the same species of wood, and are of the same thickness. One of the few precise measuring tools used in the cooper's trade is a compass, which is used to find the radius and scribe the circumference of the heads. The radius of a circle can be determined by walking off six equal steps around the circumference with a compass, because each step equals the length of the radius. First, the compass is set to an approximated radius of the opening at the bottom of the cask or bucket. Then, one point of the compass is stabbed into the wood just below the groove. From there, it is walked around the inside of the container in six steps along the groove, laying out the perimeter of an equilateral hexagon. The final step should land just short of the original stab by the exact width of the groove. It may take several adjustments to acquire an accurate measurement. The set compass can now be used to scribe the head's circumference.

All woodworkers are well acquainted with the reality that wood is not a stable material. It doesn't always play nice when you demand that it keep precise measurements. Because of this, fitting the head is an art, not a science. Long before I understood the geometry behind the measurement, I was taught how to measure heads in this way "because it works." As one fellow cooper would often say, "Don't let math confuse you." Heads are not perfect circles and they're cut to be slightly oversized to the groove. This accommodates the compression of the wood over time as the hoops are tightened, and ensures a liquid-tight fit.

Heads comprised of three or more pieces are pegged together for ease of shaping. The jointed edges are bored to receive slightly oversized square pegs made from stave offcuts. Properly jointed heading pieces create a watertight seal. On larger casks, fragments of dried river reed may be fitted in between the joints. The reed is referred to as "flagging." It's not necessary on smaller vessels, but was used copiously on repair work in the whaling industry. Dried cattail reeds work well for this.

The heads are shaped with the cooper's axe, bowsaw, and heading knife. The axe removes large amounts of material from the outer edge of the head by beveling both top and bottom. The head circumference is then rescribed and the bow saw is used to cut just outside the compass line. Finally, the beveled edges are refined to the line with the heading knife (a type of drawknife). Excess material is left on the long-grain sides of the head to allow for compression of the joints and long-term cross-grain shrinkage. This actually creates a slightly oval head.

The head of a barrel or bucket is fragile by itself, and can easily be damaged or broken if care is not taken during installation. The low hoops on the vessel must be tight prior to removing the hoops near the groove, allowing the staves to open enough to push the head into place and click into the groove. The hoops are then placed onto the container again and tightened. If the head has been shaped properly, all the joints should close up around the head and no gaps should be present.

in Motion
Dosa Attila Cooperage
Frontier
Fort McHenry

Dosa Attila Cooperage

Finishing & Hooping

Up to this point, the barrel has been built into a series of truss hoops or ring hoops. It's now time to remove these construction hoops, clean up the exterior of the cask, and replace these hoops with the final hoops. As each truss hoop is replaced, one at a time, the exterior of a cask is dressed to a smooth finish, a step done for utilitarian purposes rather than aesthetics. There are a variety of tools used to clean up the outside surface of a cask: planes, drawknives, shaves, and scrapers. I was taught to use a heavy scraper known as a "buzz."

Hoops are driven forcibly with hammer and driver from the small diameter to the large diameter, exerting a tremendous amount of force on all the staves. Whether iron, copper, hickory, or hazel, final hoops are custom-made to each container and fit at optimal points to maximize the pressure holding the vessel together. Hoops are divided into several categories: chime hoops, quarter hoops, and bouge hoops.

Metal hoops and wooden hoops evolved simultaneously throughout the history of the trade. Metal hoops, mostly iron, involved time-consuming and labor-intensive practices to mine, smelt, and form before their arrival at the cooperage; thus, they were less common until cheaper means of metal production were invented in the 19th century. While metal is durable, it's costly. Wooden hoops were inexpensive yet unreliable. Types of saplings used to bind cooperage included ash, oak, maple, walnut, hickory, hazel, and willow.

Fitting the Hoops

A piece of string is wrapped around the exterior of the barrel to measure the circumference at each location where a hoop will be fitted. The length of string is transferred to the hooping material, allowing for a sufficient amount of overlap. Cooper's hoop iron was traditionally soft wrought iron easily worked with a cold chisel and punch. In this process, the iron is cut to length at the beek/bick iron (cooper's anvil) and splayed to match the shape of the conical container. Using the straight peen of the cooper's hammer, the iron is hammered along one edge of the entire length of the strap. The hammering stretches the iron, creating the flare required to fit the piece of cooperage. The hoop is then bent by hand into the rounded shape, held onto the container for sizing and marked with chalk where a rivet is used to fasten the overlapping ends. Holes are punched into the hoop iron with the cold punch and the rivet inserted. The head of the rivet is seated inside the hoop with the shank facing outwards through the holes. The shank is then flattened and rose-headed over the anvil.

A barrel is held together primarily by the hoops. Amateur methods to seal vessels such as wax, tar, pitch, glue, or gaskets were ineffective, rarely used, and simply weren't needed by skilled coopers. All these methods fall short because correct placement of hoops and precise fitting of staves and heads are the critical factors in keeping the vessel liquid-tight.

Getting Started in Coopering

Coopering is a difficult skill to learn over just a few days, weeks, or months. With many trades, there are generally entry-level projects that are good for eager novices. While a water-tight bucket is considered the most basic vessel to make in the trade, it's extremely ambitious for a beginner. I suggest novices try their hand at making slack (dry) cooperage first. Starting on a run of slack tubs or buckets can really help to build confidence with unfamiliar tools and processes (and doesn't require firing). Don't get hung up on perfecting a single watertight vessel. You should make a number of vessels because your skills will grow from one to the next. This allows you to practice the steps of backing and hollowing staves, jointing edges, and making hoops and heads without the pressure of passing the water test. After making a half-dozen or more slack buckets, try making one that holds water.

Currently, the best institution offering classes on coopering is Tillers International in Scotts, Michigan. They offer comprehensive courses on making buckets, barrels, cooper's tools, and more. Chuck Andrews at Tillers is a dynamo of information and an amazing teacher.

Also, I suggest that those interested in learning coopering read Kenneth Kilby's book, *The Cooper and His Trade*. It's the authoritative work on traditional British coopering. Kilby outlines the method of beer barrel production and goes into detail about the European history of the trade. Colonial Williamsburg's film, "The Cooper's Craft," is a well-done narrative about the production of barrels.

Every time I make a barrel, I'm reminded of the generations of coopers who refined each motion to attain the maximum amount of leverage with minimal effort. No one person invented this trade, and I'm not even an especially talented woodworker. Rather, I consider myself a vessel of the accumulated skill that transcends generations, graciously given to me through years of instruction and consistent practice. Even now, when I take a short sabbatical from the block, I return to find my skills have atrophied and my muscles ache. Although it takes a bit to get "my hand" back into the work, practicing the ordinary dance of this craft tradition strengthens my connection to an extraordinary trade. ◆

ENDNOTES

1. Thomas Jefferson, *Thomas Jefferson's Farm Book: With Commentary and Relevant Extracts from Other Writings*, ed. Edwin Morris Betts (Princeton: Princeton University Press, 1953), 106. "The staves of a flour barrel are got 28" long & dress to 27" it takes 16-17 staves to a barrel & 6 heading pieces 22 or 23 in all. A cut of a middle sized tree yields 16 or 17 bolts, which give 4 staves each. Such a tree, midling [sic] good will yield 18 to 20 cuts. A cut will make 3 barrels, staves & heading one tree with another will make 50 barrels." And "a cooper's task is 4 flour barrels a day from the rough, i.e. from the stuff merely rived out into thicknesses for 2 staves and 6 barrels a day when the staves are drawn."
2. Clifford Ashley, *The Yankee Whaler* (London: Martin Hopkinson, 1926), 97.
3. Henry Mayhew, *The Unknown Mayhew*, eds. Eileen Yeo and E.P. Thompson (New York: Shocken, 1972), 421.
4. Virginia, *The Statutes at Large; Being a Collection of All the Laws of Virginia, from the First Session of the Legislature in the Year 1619*, ed. William Waller Hening (Charlottesville: Published for the Jamestown Foundation of the Commonwealth of Virginia by the University Press of Virginia, 1969). Vol. 2, 125, ACT CXVII. Size of Virginia Hogsheads.

"IT is enacted upon the complaint of diverse masters and merchants of ships against the incertainty and extraordinary size of caske, which hath bin very much prejudicial to them, that a certaine size of all tobacco caske of Virginia hogsheads shalbe as followeth, (vizt.) forty three inches in length and the head twenty six inches wide, with the bulge proportionable; and whoever shall make caske of a greater size shall pay upon proofe made to any court (if he be a freeman otherwise his master or mistris that imploys him) three thousand pounds of tobacco, the one halfe to the informer, the other halfe to the county where the caske is made; and if any caske shalbe made of timber not seasoned, then such caske to be burnt."

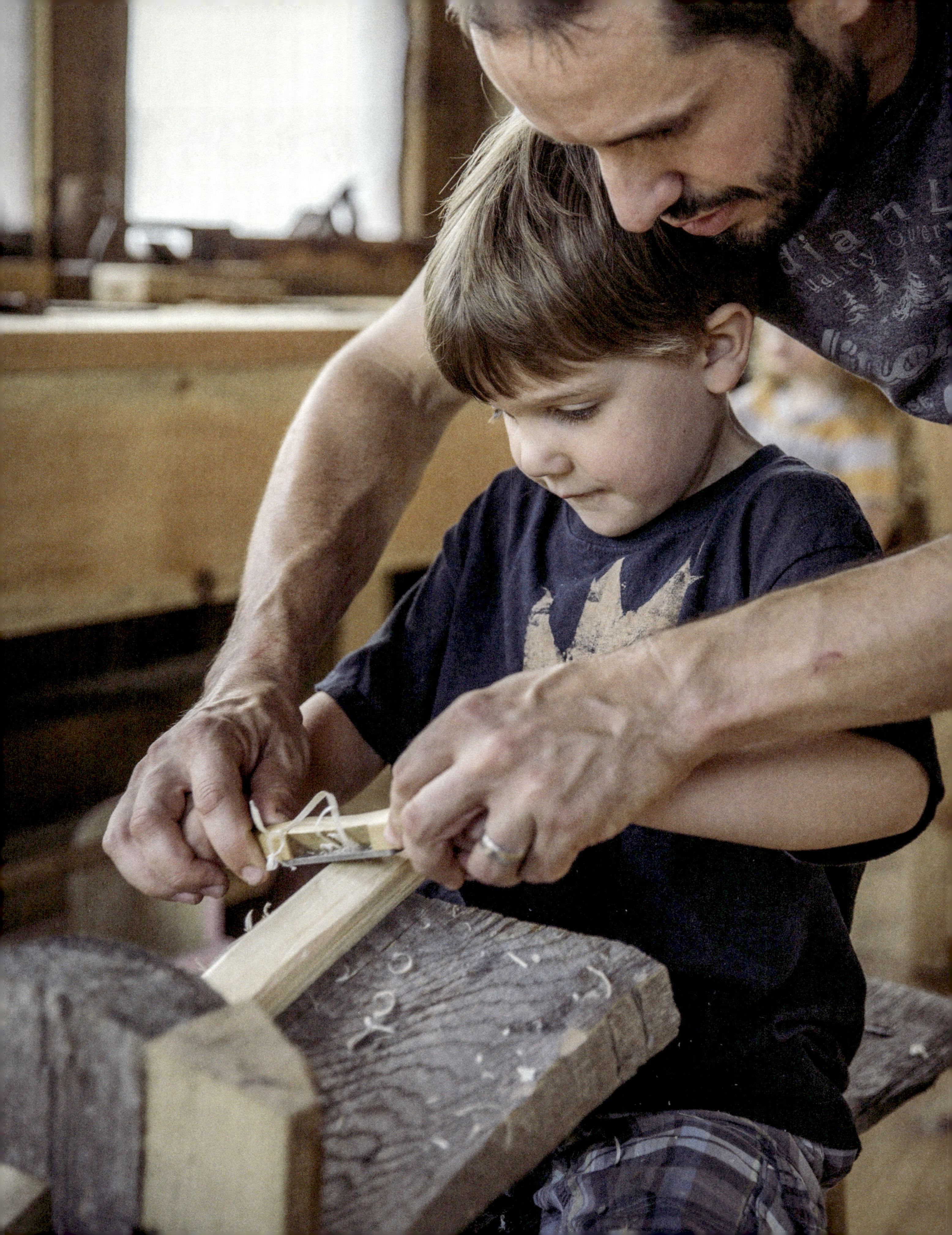

TOOLS FOR LEARNING
Woodworking with Young Children

Joshua A. Klein & Michael Updegraff

> "Work is one of the primary means whereby a child learns, grows, feels a sense of belonging, and discovers ways of being a useful member of society.... [It] is one of our most useful learning tools; children love to imitate adults at work."
> – William Coperthwaite, *A Handmade Life*

Children are hard-wired to create. Any parent who has discovered a fort made of couch cushions, waded through a pile of Legos, or swept bits of paper, glitter, and dried glue knows this well. When kids are offered time in a full-blown woodshop, most leap at the opportunity.

Our children need to learn to work with their hands. They need the freedom to work in the shop, to saw boards (with real saws), and nail together whatever they can dream up. When kids learn to work wood they develop manual dexterity, yes. But more than that, woodworking is an opportunity to cultivate the patience, discipline, and independence that distinguishes a well-balanced individual.

These experiences often have lasting effects. Most every veteran woodworker can tell childhood stories about their time in their father's or their uncle's workshop, let loose to bang nails into boards. They often credit this experience with setting them on a life-long trajectory of making things with their own hands.

In the 21st century, this kind of opportunity is not a given. It's common knowledge that in the United States, "shop class" has been almost now entirely removed from public education. In its place, a lopsided emphasis on STEM (science, technology, engineering, and math) divests children of a well-rounded educational experience. Though they can navigate iPads with ease and code their way into the future, studies suggest that all of that screen time and cerebral work threatens loss of dexterity, even that which is needed to hold a pencil.[1]

So, what are we to do if our children are no longer taught to work with their hands? How can we as mentors and parents fill this gap in their educational experience?

An Old Solution

This is not a new problem. In 19th-century Sweden, an educator and writer named Otto Salomon identified similar inadequacies in the educational

Long cut. | To cut off a piece of wood in the direction of the length of the fibres.

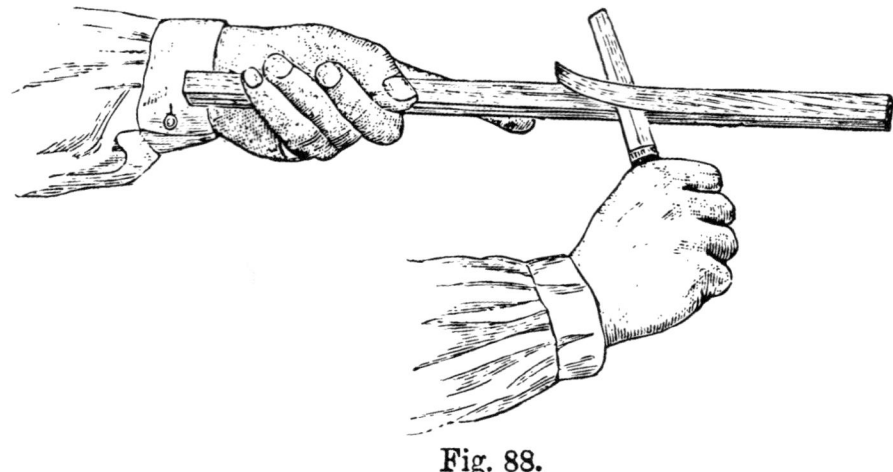

Fig. 88.

system of his day. Salomon believed the schools taught only at a superficial level and failed to touch the hearts of their pupils. His answer was a system he called "educational slöjd" – "slöjd" is a Swedish word that means "craft."

Salomon wrote, "[The aim of educational slöjd is] to utilize…the educative force which lies directly in bodily labour." He said that by its exercise, children develop "pleasure in bodily labour, and respect for it, habits of independence, order, accuracy, attention and industry, increase of physical strength, development of the power of observation in the eye and of the execution in the hand. Educational slöjd has also in view the development of mental power, or in other words, is disciplinary in its aim."[2] He stressed that "the principal object is not the article made, but the mental and physical benefits which accrue to the pupil by means of the work."[3]

This slöjd system is still used in Scandinavian public education today. But what about the rest of us without an educational system that values handcraft? If we want the next generation to learn these fundamental skills, it is up to us as mentors and parents.

In the slöjd system, the youngest children start out with origami-like paper projects, waiting to begin learning woodworking techniques until around 10 years of age. This makes certain sense as sharp tools require a good degree of physical and cognitive development to use effectively. However, we wondered if there is a kind of woodworking that can be done with our littlest kids that can lay the groundwork for the slöjd-type learning they will receive in their later years.

We've experimented with different ways of doing "shop time" with our kids, to varying degrees of success. Because – let's be honest – working with kids in your shop is not always an idyllic experience. There have been times of frustration, tantrums, and fizzled projects, but we've both seen the value of this time invested and are encouraged by every step of growth. It still amazes us that, despite our own failures, our kids began to hold and use tools when they were in diapers.

A Lesson Relearned

I (Mike) recently had the opportunity to demonstrate hand-tool woodworking to school-age children at a medieval fair. I'd gone into the event planning on providing several workstations where various tasks could be tried – a shaving horse with spokeshaves, a workbench for planing, and even a spring-pole lathe. While I'd prepared to lecture on the ancient guild system and the

Continued on page 72

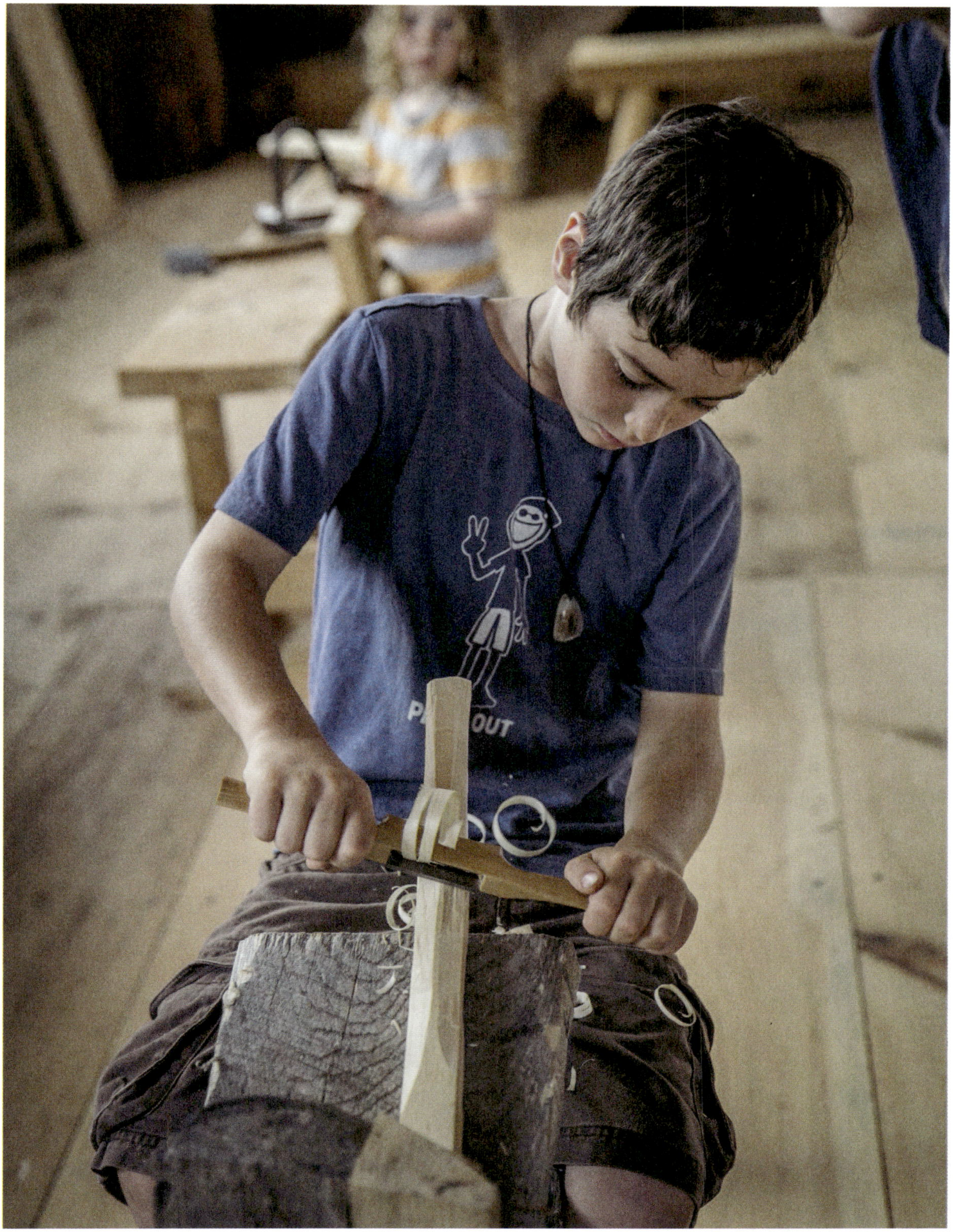

Orthographic Projection   Greek Ornament

Plane the face
Plane the edge
gauge to width
gauge to thickness

Postcard of schoolboys in woodworking class circa 1900-1910.
Probably Yorkshire, U.K.

apprenticeship model of learning a trade, my young visitors just wanted to make stuff – specifically, swords. Before I realized what had happened, the kids' creative demands overthrew all my teaching points and, soon, blades were being tapered on the planing bench and sharpened on the shaving horse. Many children left the woodworking booth that day proudly brandishing their gleaming Excalibur sword-sticks. This lesson, that great satisfaction is found in making an object with your own hands, can be life-changing.

I was reminded that day just how easy it is to sneak in valuable educational morsels when everyone is having fun. As furniture maker and teacher Reid Beverly has noted, "Anecdotes, history, silly stories, a math lesson, and shop lore can all serve as brain food while kids are working through exercises. A carefully chosen story can provide the connective sinew between what the child is practicing and the wider universe."[4] Young kids are sponges for information, and when they are given the chance to process new words and ideas experientially, rather than passively, those lessons will stick.

The Trivium & The Toolbox

Experiential learning is nothing new – it was the foundation of Western educational theory from ancient times into the 20th century. Early Greek philosophers and teachers envisaged virtuous citizens who were able to think critically for themselves. Character building was considered a central tenet of this philosophy, just as it was in Salomon's "slöjd" method much later. Rather than just a means of receiving subject matter, Classical Education, as the model is now called, was designed to teach children the art of learning, imparted to the youngest students through song, story, and play.

At the core of the Classical method was the trivium, a progressive three-stage cycle intended to deepen knowledge in any given area of study. Oxford scholar and Classical Method advocate Dorothy Sayers said that "the whole of the Trivium was, in fact, intended to teach the pupil the proper use of the tools of learning, before he began to apply them to 'subjects' at all."[5] Equipping children with these educational "tools" began at a very young age.

The Grammar Stage of Woodworking

The three stages of the trivium correspond to the age and learning ability of the student. In the first, or "grammar" stage, when young children are sponges for names, places, and stories, the terminology of a subject is taught. Just as in learning a foreign language, the key is immersion.

To teach grammar in the subject of woodworking, we might sit a young child on a shaving horse and mention the various parts – he or she will giggle if you have a "dumbhead"-style. Be intentional about sharing the language: "spokeshave," "treadle," "ash," "oak." Let them repeat the words, growing familiar with them as they work. Kids are often content to make shavings almost endlessly, but this is not the stage to teach the production of perfectly dimensioned spindles for Windsor chairs. At the grammar stage, they become comfortable and familiar with the tools, the names of techniques, kinds of joinery, and the sheer fun of shaping wood, even with no particular end in mind.

Mike saw this when his youngest son, at three years old, took interest in backsaws. He enjoyed hunting flea markets with his dad in search of them, and when he discovered a tenon saw amidst dull and bent crosscuts, he would shout for joy. Of course, he had no idea of the function of the tool and had no ability to use or maintain it, but he could instantly recognize the form. This familiarity is the seed of a deeper understanding.

The Slöjd Stage

At around 10 years of age, a student enters what was historically called the dialectic (or logic) stage – for our purposes,

Detail from "The School of Athens" by Raffaello Sanzio da Urbino. From Wikimedia Commons.

we'll call it the slöjd stage. At this point, they begin to move beyond the basics, from identifying "what" to asking "how?" and "why?" Slöjd students begin to ask tougher questions about woodworking technique, to answer back and contradict, and to form their own opinions about how to do things. (Sayers says of this stage, "Its nuisance-value is extremely high."[6])

Rather than simply driving nails into a piece of firewood, kids of this age want to tackle a project – and they begin to apply logic and reason (designing and planning) to that end. This is the time to take the grammar of tools and techniques and put them into practice. Instead of blissfully shaving boards and staves down to nothingness, we begin to teach them process – to shape wood with an end in mind. Basic joinery can be introduced, with its controlled cuts and careful sawing. When the tools are familiar and the language has been learned, kids can begin crafting their own projects.

Instead of teaching a child the step-by-step method of making a specific object, it is often more beneficial in the long run to permit a bit more experimentation. Allowing the pursuit of a flawed idea, even to the point of failure, can be a tremendous learning experience. Failures lead to specific questions, and the answers to these questions can be far more enlightening than the rote knowledge found in a pre-packaged step project. Sayers again: "The pupils should be encouraged to go and forage for their own information, and so guided towards the proper use of libraries and books for reference, and shown how to tell which sources are authoritative and which are not."[7] If they haven't met Roy Underhill yet, now is the time.

The Self-sufficiency Stage: The Goal of the Trivium

The final stage of the trivium (which we should all desire to attain) is called the "rhetoric" stage, or, for our purposes, self-sufficiency. Once the language of woodworking has been learned, once tools and techniques have become comfortable and practiced, once the strengths and weaknesses of the materials of the craft are understood, the child can be set free to create with confidence. In philosophical studies, this means that a thesis can be composed and logically defended. In woodworking, it means any project can be assessed and executed. At this stage, the child can fill any gaps in craft knowledge independently, because the tools of learning have been honed to a keen edge.

Age-appropriate Activities

It is important to assess your children's abilities when you bring them into the shop. For reasons of safety and success, you'll need to discern how responsive they are to directions, especially with the older children who will be given sharp edge tools. If you are working with a child who has a degree of self-awareness and is quick to respond to adult direction (the maturity that Salomon was looking for), he or she can be entrusted with sharp tools.

Some tools and activities are more safe than others for children at the "grammar" stage, and we have put together a list of suggestions below. Every kid is different; there are no infallible recommendations so judgement comes into play. As Salomon reminds us, shop time is just as much about personal development as it is hand-skill development, so this time in the shop with our kids is a time for us grow in our understanding of their strengths and weaknesses and provide them with the tools and guidance to blossom into strong, healthy individuals. You cannot mentally check out and simply hand your kid tools to play with – you've got to stay engaged and available. The following list generally describes how we've introduced our kids to woodworking tools.

One-year-olds – Wooden play tools are a great first birthday gift. These allow them to develop a feel for holding tools and begin to imitate woodworking techniques they see adults and older siblings doing. A soft wood mallet, a wooden saw, and a workbench with holes to drive pegs are an excellent start. At this age – especially if there are older siblings – a one-year-old will often develop a sense of proud ownership of his or her tools. There will be squabbles with siblings over who took whose stuff but this is a great opportunity to teach children to develop responsibility for their own tools and respect of others'.

Two- to four-year-olds – Nails, nails, nails. At this age all they want is a hammer and a pile of nails. Hammering is a great introduction to woodworking because careful attention and aim are required for success, but the bar is relatively low and the results are instantaneous. In our experience, two-year-olds have an attention span of about 20 seconds, so hitting nails into pine scraps is perfect. At this age, we've introduced our kids to sawing with a crosscut handsaw, but only with hands-on supervision. We put our hands over theirs on the handle to teach them to feel when the saw is moving freely in the kerf. We've also found they can use rasps safely, but be aware that all tools tend to become hammers at this age.

"Passion and enthusiasm are contagious. The teacher has a lot to do with student motivation – if it's in the teacher from the start, it will spread."

– Edward Bouvier, *Village Woodwright, Inc.* Chicago, Ill.

Five-year-olds – Joshua made his oldest son a fully functional kid-sized workbench for his fifth Christmas. This bench has remained in the front entry hall of the house so that all the kids can work at it whenever they want. At five years old, our kids have been given their own hammers, tape measures, squares, rasps, coping saws, handsaws, marking gauges, and screwdrivers, as well as their first handplane.

Six- to nine-year-olds – If a six-year-old has been swinging a hammer since the age of two, he or she is often competent to build simple things without help. We give kids at this stage a pile of nails and let them make whatever excites them. Usually, it is a category-bending semi-mechanical abstract contraption unrecognizable to adults. (Children are not yet fettered by convention.) You cannot encourage them enough. Marvel at their ingenuity and furnish them with compliments.

Knives, chisels, and hatchets are slöjd-stage tools and are therefore best reserved for children exhibiting the most-developed physical ability, respect for sharp edges, and awareness of themselves and their surroundings. These tools should never be handed over to a small child to store in their own personal tool chest as they require attentive adult supervision.

Practical Advice

Let them have fun so that they develop positive experiences in the shop. This is the number-one goal when bringing young kids into the workshop – to get them enthusiastic about making. Focus and attention span are often lacking in today's littlest students, so care should be taken to walk that difficult tightrope between challenge and boredom. Once boredom sets in, it will be difficult to reclaim your audience. And, yes, safety is always important, but make sure to keep the atmosphere light so that the experience does not cripple their creativity. A crude project, assembled in minutes, will often encourage and inspire further exploration. As they mature, they will be able to handle more woodworking operations and tackle increasingly complex projects.

Give kids quality, sharp tools. We all know how frustrating it is to work with dull tools – don't do that to your kids. If you put a real tool in their hands, they'll get real results and the urge to create will become insatiable. But it should go without saying that small children and dangerous woodworking machinery are incompatible. Keep kids away from machines.

Be sensitive to each child's individual needs and abilities in order to provide an environment for growth and success. Some kids thrive on following explicit directions while others would rather blaze their own trail. Work with their strengths and gently support their weaknesses, all with the aim of fostering a positive and creative shop experience. Succeed in this and they'll be set on a trajectory of making.

Make them a kid-sized worksurface. It doesn't have to be fancy but don't make your kids climb on a chair to reach your 34"-tall workbench top. You know how impossible it would be for you to work at eye level. It takes only a few minutes to bang together a simple 2x4 bench. Set them up for success.

Practice creative generosity. Children are naturally imaginative in their gift-giving. From crayon drawings to daisy chains, kids love making things to give away and be appreciated. This bent toward creative expression can be nurtured by setting an example for our children to follow in this area. By giving thoughtful handmade gifts, you demonstrate a compellingly beautiful way to unplug from a culture of consumerism. Simple nailed wooden boxes, with parts cut beforehand, are great gifts for young kids to make and offer wonderful opportunities to guide creative instinct.

But, let go of your own high standards of workmanship. To put it lightly, kids' work tends to be a little rough around the edges. There will be dents from hammer blows, scars from errant saw teeth, and blowout from nails. These are their fingerprints of craftsmanship. If it's important to have a clean surface after the kids' nailing, set the heads and smooth it after assembly.

Tools for Learning: A Meaningful Tradition

Picasso famously said, "Every child is an artist. The problem is how to remain an artist once he grows up." His point was that kids usually come to a place when the confidence they have in their ability to draw or create dwindles. This usually coincides with the end of the grammar stage, when the ability to compare work critically emerges. The joy of creating can become a frustrating endeavour as the desire to reach a perceived standard bumps up against skill limits. If artistic growth is not fostered, that spark can be extinguished in a child. We must fight against this trend.

Intentionally engaging in handcraft with children offers tremendous positive benefit for everyone. It's been said that if you can't explain a concept to a six-year-old, you don't understand it yourself. Distilling a skillful operation down to basic terms can turn the lights on for us as well as our young audience. Children delight in asking "why?," while we as adults perhaps don't ask that question enough. Why do we cut tails first? Why do we hold our chisel that way? We realize how much we don't know when confronted with a simple, innocent inquiry.

Most of us treasure those childhood memories of time spent in the shop or in a garage with an adult who showed us some novel skill for the first time. Whether whittling with an old pocketknife or building a birdhouse, these early craft lessons stick. The relational value of these times can be immense, and regular shop time with our kids is a wonderful way to nurture them and deepen our bonds.

This passing on of skills from one generation to the next is a powerful, meaningful tradition, and in those intentional times we can teach more than the basics of woodworking. We can instill the values of making objects that are lasting and beautiful, being disciplined in the pursuit of excellence, and focusing on the tangible more than the virtual. These values will serve our kids well as they grow into adulthood and navigate the turbulent waters of this quickly changing world. ◆

ENDNOTES

1. https://www.theguardian.com/society/2018/feb/25/children-struggle-to-hold-pencils-due-to-too-much-tech-doctors-say (accessed July 2, 2018)
2. Otto Salomon, *The Teacher's Hand-book of Slöjd*, (Boston, New York, Chicago: Silver Burdett & Co., 1891), 2.
3. Ibid., 15.
4. Reid Beverly, email message to authors, July 8, 2018.
5. Dorothy Sayers, "The Lost Tools of Learning" (Lecture, Oxford University, 1947. http://www.gbt.org/text/sayers.html).
6. Ibid.
7. Ibid.

"However firmly a tradition is rooted, if it is never watered, though it dies hard, yet in the end it dies. ... We have lost the tools of learning – the axe and the wedge, the hammer and the saw, the chisel and the plane – that were so adaptable to all tasks. Instead of them, we have merely a set of complicated jigs, each of which will do but one task and no more, and in using which eye and hand receive no training, so that no man ever sees the work as a whole. ... For the sole true end of education is simply this: to teach [children] how to learn for themselves; and whatever instruction fails to do this is effort spent in vain."

– Dorothy Sayers

Steel engraving from 1881, showing Robinson Crusoe building a wooden boat with tools scavenged from the shipwreck. (Getty Images)

Woodworking in Classic Literature

Megan Fitzpatrick

We should all take craft (and life) lessons from Robinson Crusoe: with just a few tools and no woodworking experience, he built two homes, the furniture therein, and several watercraft from both reclaimed lumber and logs, and managed to live a reasonably happy and healthy 28 years on a mostly unpeopled tropical island.

While Daniel Defoe's 1719 novel (by some considered the first novel written in English) jars modern sensibilities by airing the societal mores of the day (including religious exclusivity and slavery), for woodworkers, it's of special interest because of the tools and Crusoe's use thereof. After being shipwrecked (for the second time) about 40 miles off the coast of Brazil, Crusoe makes several trips to the wreck to salvage what he can, and begins by building a raft:

"We had several spare yards, and two or three large spars of wood, and a spare topmast or two in the ship; I resolved to fall to work with these, and I flung as many of them overboard as I could manage for their weight, tying every one with a rope, that they might not drive away. When this was done I went down the ship's side, and pulling them to me, I tied four of them together at both ends as well as I could, in the form of a raft, and laying two or three short pieces of plank upon them crossways, I found I could walk upon it very well, but that it was not able to bear any great weight, the pieces being too light. So I went to work, and with a carpenter's saw I cut a spare topmast into three lengths, and added them to my raft, with a great deal of labour and pains."[1]

First, he loads his craft with salvaged boards (he is perhaps also the first fictional English upcycler), food, clothing, and alcohol, then he goes for the tools, knowing how important they'd be to his survival: "…I had other things which my eye was more upon—as, first, tools to work with on shore. And it was after long searching that I found out the carpenter's chest, which was, indeed, a very useful prize to me, and much more valuable than a shipload of gold would have been at that time. I got it down to my raft, whole as it was, without losing time to look into it, for I knew in general what it contained."[2]

How did this plantation owner and trader know what tools would be in the chest? Defoe doesn't say – but Crusoe, despite having been bred to no trade (as we learn in Chapter 1), is quite familiar with tools themselves, if not altogether competent in their use (as is later revealed):

"But yet I brought away several things very useful to me; as first, in the carpenters stores I found two or three bags full of nails and spikes, a great screw-jack, a dozen or two of hatchets, and, above all, that most useful thing called a grindstone."[3] (A grindstone is, as we know, indeed most useful, though later evidence suggests Crusoe doesn't actually know how to use it.)

The first structure he builds is a staked palisade to protect himself and his salvaged goods from "savages" and wild animals, with a ladder he can pull over the top to keep people from climbing in while he's behind it inside a convenient cave. Next, he builds a calendar of sorts – a wooden cross, the upright into which he notches the passage of each day. Into the horizontal member, he carves "I came on shore here on the 30th September 1659."[4]

After a period of building palisade additions – plus a bit of rock carving to enlarge his cave (no mention of the tools used there) – Crusoe starts to furnish his home, for he cannot, he says, take enjoyment in his few comforts of writing and eating without a table and chair. And he displays a bit of false modesty in the process:

"And here I must needs observe, that as reason is the substance and origin of the mathematics, so by stating and squaring everything by reason, and by making the most rational judgment of things, every man may be, in time, master of every mechanic art. I had never handled a tool in my life; and yet, in time, by labour, application, and contrivance, I found at last that I wanted nothing but I could have made it, especially if I had had tools. However, I made abundance of things, even without tools; and some with no more tools than an adze and a hatchet, which perhaps were never made that way before, and that with infinite labour. For example, if I wanted a board, I had no other way but to cut down a tree, set it on an edge before me, and hew it flat on either side with my axe, till I brought it to be thin as a plank, and then dub it smooth with my adze. It is true, by this method I could make but one board out of a whole tree; but this I had no remedy for but patience, any more than I had for the prodigious deal of time and labour which it took me up to make a plank or board: but my time or labour was little worth, and so it was as well employed one way as another."[5]

While he does, with time and effort, become a rude mechanic, it's a shame Crusoe (or his creator) didn't figure out how to split a log with the axe and make better use of his resources. While Defoe championed the English tradesman as a bedrock of the English economy and argued in *The Complete English Tradesman* (1726) that most men are by experience, marriage, or history linked to trade, he was, it seems, lacking in knowledge of the particulars of joiner's work.

"However, I made me a table and a chair, as I observed above, in the first place; and this I did out of the short pieces of boards that I brought on my raft from the ship. But when I had wrought out some boards as above, I made large shelves, of the breadth of a foot and a half, one over another all along one side of my cave, to lay all my tools, nails and ironwork on; and, in a word, to separate everything at large into their places, that I might come easily at them. I knocked pieces into the wall of the rock to hang my guns and all things that would hang up; so that, had my cave been to be seen, it looked like a general magazine of all necessary things; and had everything so ready at my hand, that it was a great pleasure to me to see all my goods in such order, and especially to find my stock of all necessaries so great."[6]

As he begins to keep a post-dated diary (until his ink runs out), Crusoe reveals a bit more about his woodworking, his toolkit, and his cleverness in keeping it in working order.

"Dec. 20. – Now I carried everything into the cave, and began to furnish my house, and set up some pieces of boards like a dresser, to order my victuals upon; but boards began to be very scarce with me; also, I made me another table."[7]

So perhaps not too scarce.

"April 22. – The next morning I begin to consider of means to put this resolve into execution; but I was at a great loss about my tools. I had three large axes, and abundance of hatchets (for we carried the hatchets for traffic with the Indians); but with much chopping and cutting knotty hard wood [there is what he calls "iron-wood" on the island], they were all full of notches, and dull; and though I had a grindstone, I could not turn it and grind my tools too. This cost me as much thought as a statesman would have bestowed upon a grand point of politics, or a judge upon the life and death of a man. At length I contrived a wheel with a string, to turn it with my foot, that I might have both my hands at liberty. Note. – I had never seen any such thing in England, or at least, not to take notice how it was done, though since I have observed, it is very common there; besides that, my grindstone was very large and heavy. This machine cost me a full week's work to bring it to perfection.

"April 28, 29. – These two whole days I took up in grinding my tools, my machine for turning my grindstone performing very well."[8]

Years later, after he rescues from cannibals the man who becomes his servant, Friday, it's clear that Crusoe has kept his woodworking skills up to snuff, building "a formal framed door-case, and a door to it, of boards, and set it up in the passage, a little within the entrance; and, causing the door to open in the inside, I barred it up in the night, taking in my ladders, too."[9]

It was, as he later reveals, wholly unnecessary, for never has there been a more devoted friend and servant than the (ill-used) Friday, whom Crusoe treats alternately as a servant and child (sometimes to the point of idiocy). While this paternalistic attitude is exemplified in many passages, it is particularly clear when, in Chapter 16, they build a boat to rescue some Europeans taken captive by the cannibals who sometimes visit the island. Despite Friday's experience with the regional timber and island craft, Crusoe imposes his European tools and standards on the process:

"At last Friday pitched upon a tree; for I found he knew much better than I what kind of wood was fittest for it; nor can I tell to this day what wood to call the tree we cut down, except that it was very like the tree we call fustic, or between that and the Nicaragua wood, for it was much of the same colour and smell. Friday wished to burn the hollow or cavity of this tree out, to make it for a boat, but I showed him how to cut it with tools; which, after I had showed him how to use, he did very handily; and in about a month's hard labour we finished it and made it very handsome; especially when, with our axes, which I showed him how to handle, we cut and hewed the outside into the true shape of a boat."[10]

I've never burned out the entire interior of an 8' log – but the many instructions available indicate that a slow, controlled burn over several hours allows an adze to make quick work of about 2"-3" of charcoal removal, then repeat. Surely that's more efficient than dull steel alone.

Yet despite the many passages uncomfortable to modern sensibilities, Defoe's *Robinson Crusoe* is at least in part a testament to the fact that anyone can learn to work wood – even a kid from Hull with no experience and training, and no teacher. All it takes is tools, time, and a healthy dollop of ego. And perhaps necessity.

Most of the woodworking mentioned in classic works of fiction and drama aren't as integral to character development or plot (or survival) as in *Crusoe*, yet there are mentions of craft scattered throughout a handful of fairly well-known works (and some lesser-known ones) that serve different purposes.

Above I mentioned that Crusoe taught himself to be a "rude mechanic" – a term that sounds derogatory…and sort of is, at least in Shakespeare.

A "rude mechanic" is an early modern term for a skilled laborer – at the time, typically a man – who worked with his hands in some form of trade associated with making things, be that buildings or furniture. Today, we might term that same maker a craftsman/craftsperson or artisan – terms lacking in the now-pejorative "rude" (meaning uneducated).

There are six "rude mechanicals" in the circa-1595 "A Midsummer Night's Dream" – a group of craftsmen who perform "Pyramus and Thisbe" (the play within the play) for the king and queen and other elite of Athens, and they are presented as bumbling fools.

But why are tradesmen performing for royalty? It's an activity that has its basis in the medieval period. In England (and other countries, but I'm most familiar with English history), from sometime in the 14th century (when the clergy and monks ceded the stage) up until not too long before William Shakespeare was born (1564), "theater" consisted solely of "traveling" religious pageants ("mystery plays" or "mystery cycles") that were acted by a city's guilds. Each guild would present a pageant within the cycle, and that guild made the props and owned the costumes, which would be used year after year.

In the York cycle, for example (one of a handful of cycles that survive almost in their entirety), we know that every year on Corpus Christi day, the Shipwright's Guild presented the building of the ark, the Goldsmiths staged the "Adoration," the Bakers' Guild did the "Last Supper," and the Carpenter's Guild presented the "Resurrection."

By Shakespeare's time, plays were no longer restricted to religious topics, and there were a couple of professional playhouses and theater companies in London by the time he was an adult. But a group of "rude mechanicals" wanting to stage a play (within a play) would be within living memory for some theater goers, and would be recognized as a quaint, old-fashioned undertaking – ha ha…look at the backward craftsmen! And yes, Shakespeare presented most of his rude mechanicals as just a bit lacking in brains. They are:

• Nick Bottom, a weaver. He wants to play all the parts (a bit of an inside theater joke, given that his is the one major role that can't be doubled – that is, have the same actor play more than one part, because he's in two many scenes), and eventually gets turned into an actual ass, then back (to a merely metaphoric ass).

• Peter Quince, a carpenter. The group's leader; he chooses the play "Pyramus and Thisbe," assigns the roles and delivers the prologue. The play is dreadful – a tragedy performed (not on purpose) as wholly comedic.

• Francis Flute, the bellows mender. He is dismayed to be playing Thisbe, a lady.

• Tom Snout, a tinker. He plays Thisbe's father…and also portrays a wall (which affords much mirth due to crude jokes about holes), because the group can't afford to build props, despite their presumed skill at making things.

• Robin Starveling, a tailor. He plays the moon, with a lantern in hand.

• Snug, a joiner. He plays a lion. Snug is a little on the slow side, but he's a kind soul; he's concerned that the

Louis Rhead's illustration of Snug the Joiner, from a 1918 edition of Charles and Mary Lamb's *Tales from Shakespeare*.

Detail of Wenceslaus Hollar's 1647 etching "Long View of London from Bankside," copied in part from Claes Jansz Visscher's 1616 panorama, with a notable mistake: the building labeled "The Globe" is the Hope Theatre; the larger circular building labeled "Beere bayting" is The Globe, as it was rebuilt following a fire. (Public domain image; the original is in the collection of the British Museum.)

women in the audience will be scared of him in his lion guise:

"You, ladies, you, whose gentle hearts do fear
The smallest monstrous mouse that creeps on floor,
May now perchance both quake and tremble here,
When lion rough in wildest rage doth roar.
Then know that I, one Snug the joiner, am
A lion-fell, nor else no lion's dam;
For, if I should as lion come in strife
Into this place, 'twere pity on my life."[11]

By writing the rude mechanicals as fools, Shakespeare is possibly poking fun at the craft of playing; as far as we know, most early modern actors came from families in the trades or lower on the social ladder. Or, more likely, he's showing that even the meanest among us can become kings (if only on stage). Among the backgrounds of the original actors in Shakespeare's company (the Lord Chamberlain's Men, later the King's Men) that we know or can guess, evidence points toward Henry Condell as being the son of a Norwich fishmonger, John Heminge was apprenticed for nine years to a grocer (and stayed active in the grocer's guild alongside his acting career), Shakespeare himself was the son of a glover, Richard Burbage was the son of a joiner — which served him well when in 1599, the company dismantled the timber-framed Theatre in Shoreditch following a dispute with the site's landowner, and moved it across the Thames (legend has it in the dead of night, over frozen river ice) where it was reconstructed it as The Globe in Southwark.

Jump forward a few hundred years, and a titular craftsman is portrayed not as a bumbler, but as a trustworthy, honorable man in George Eliot's 1859 novel *Adam Bede*. In Chapter 19, the author lauds Adam and the working class:

"He was not an average man. Yet such men as he are reared here and there in every generation of our peasant artisans — with an inheritance of affections nurtured by a simple family life of common need and common industry, and an inheritance of faculties trained in skilful courageous labour: they make their way upwards, rarely as geniuses, most commonly as painstaking honest men, with the skill and conscience to do well the tasks that lie before them. Their lives have no discernible echo beyond the neighbourhood where they dwelt, but you are almost sure to find there some good piece of road, some building, some application of mineral produce, some improvement in farming practice, some reform of parish abuses, with which their names are associated by one or two generations after them. Their employers were the richer for them, the work of their hands has worn well, and the work of their brains has guided well the hands of other men. They went about in their youth in flannel or paper caps, in coats black with coal-dust or streaked with lime and red paint; in old age their white hairs are seen in a place of honour at church and at market, and they tell their well-dressed sons and daughters, seated round the bright hearth on winter evenings, how pleased they were when they first earned their twopence a-day. Others there are who die poor and never put off the workman's coat on weekdays. They have not had the art of getting rich, but they are men of trust, and when they die before the work is all out of them, it is as if some main screw had got loose in a machine; the master who employed them says, "Where shall I find their like?"[12]

The book opens with a view of the shop, of which Adam is foreman, as the men discuss religion and finish the day's work:

"I will show you the roomy workshop of Mr. Jonathan Burge, carpenter and builder, in the village of Hayslope, as it appeared on the eighteenth of June, in the year of our Lord 1799.

"The afternoon sun was warm on the five workmen there, busy upon doors and window-frames and wainscoting. A scent of pine-wood from a tentlike pile of planks outside the open door mingled itself with the scent of the elder-bushes which were spreading their summer snow close to the open window opposite; the slanting sunbeams shone through

ADAM BEDE.

The frontispiece to an 1893 edition of *Adam Bede*.
Engraving by Frank T. Merrill.

The frontispiece to an 1898 edition of *Jack Shepperd*.

the transparent shavings that flew before the steady plane, and lit up the fine grain of the oak panelling which stood propped against the wall. On a heap of those soft shavings a rough, grey shepherd dog had made himself a pleasant bed, and was lying with his nose between his fore-paws, occasionally wrinkling his brows to cast a glance at the tallest of the five workmen, who was carving a shield in the centre of a wooden mantelpiece. It was to this workman that the strong barytone belonged which was heard above the sound of plane and hammer singing—

"Awake, my soul, and with the sun
Thy daily stage of duty run;
Shake off dull sloth...

"Here some measurement was to be taken which required more concentrated attention, and the sonorous voice subsided into a low whistle; but it presently broke out again with renewed vigour—

"Let all thy converse be sincere,
Thy conscience as the noonday clear.

"Such a voice could only come from a broad chest, and the broad chest belonged to a large-boned, muscular man nearly six feet high, with a back so flat and a head so well poised that when he drew himself up to take a more distant survey of his work, he had the air of a soldier standing at ease. The sleeve rolled up above the elbow showed an arm that was likely to win the prize for feats of strength; yet the long supple hand, with its broad finger-tips, looked ready for works of skill. In his tall stalwartness Adam Bede was a Saxon, and justified his name; but the jet-black hair, made the more noticeable by its contrast with the light paper cap, and the keen glance of the dark eyes that shone from under strongly marked, prominent and mobile eyebrows, indicated a mixture of Celtic blood. The face was large and roughly hewn, and when in repose had no other beauty than such as belongs to an expression of good-humoured honest intelligence."[13]

Seth Bede, however, is not as fortunate in face or work ethic, and he's distracted from building a paneled door by thoughts of the woman preacher he admires. He's forgotten to put the panels in place, and a discussion on religion ensues. I don't know about you, but I'm not usually musing on the Bible as I build. But Adam, honest and reliable craftsman that he is, finds religion in his work.

"But what does the Bible say? Why, it says as God put his sperrit into the workman as built the tabernacle, to make him do all the carved work and things as wanted a nice hand. And this is my way o' looking at it: there's the sperrit o' God in all things and all times – weekday as well as Sunday – and i' the great works and inventions, and i' the figuring and the mechanics. And God helps us with our headpieces and our hands as well as with our souls; and if a man does bits o' jobs out o' working hours – builds a oven for 's wife to save her from going to the bakehouse, or scrats at his bit o' garden and makes two potatoes grow istead o' one, he's doin' more good, and he's just as near to God, as if he was running after some preacher and a-praying and a-groaning."[14]

I do find fulfillment in working with my hands – so in that, at least, I agree with young Adam.

Adam Bede could be any rural artisan, really – his specific craft isn't as important as the "type" Eliot draws by the portrayal of the honest and hardworking craftsman. But references abound in the book (a romantic novel of rural life and lives) to tools and their care. Adam Bede is the very model of an English artisan.

The opposite is portrayed in William Harrison Ainsworth's *Jack Sheppard*, which was published serially in *Bentley's Miscellaney*, and in three-volume book form in 1839. He's not exactly the apprentice one might want in any trade, but thanks to his training we get a view of the shop... then see what Jack is doing in it.

"One Friday afternoon, in this pleasant month, it chanced that Mr. Wood, who had been absent on business during the greater part of the day, returned (perhaps not altogether undesignedly) at an earlier hour than was expected, to his dwelling in Wych Street, Drury Lane; and was about to enter his workshop, when, not hearing any sound of labour issue from within, he began to suspect that an apprentice, of whose habits of industry he entertained some doubt, was neglecting his employment. Impressed with this idea, he paused for a moment to listen. But finding all continue silent, he cautiously lifted the latch, and crept into the room, resolved to punish the offender in case his suspicions should prove correct.

"The chamber, into which he stole, like all carpenters' workshops, was crowded with the implements and materials of that ancient and honourable art. Saws, hammers, planes, axes, augers, adzes, chisels, gimblets [sic], and an endless variety of tools were ranged, like a stand of martial weapons at an armoury, in racks against the walls. Over these hung levels, bevels, squares, and other instruments of measurement. Amid a litter of nails without heads, screws without worms, and locks without wards, lay a glue-pot and an oilstone, two articles which their owner was wont to term 'his right hand and his left.' On a shelf was placed a row of paint-jars; the contents of which had been daubed in rainbow streaks upon the adjacent closet and window sill. Divers plans and figures were chalked upon the walls. ... The floor was thickly strewn with sawdust and shavings; and across the room ran a long and wide bench, furnished at one end with a powerful vice; next to which three nails driven into the boards served, it would appear from the lump of unconsumed tallow left in their custody, as a substitute for a candlestick. On the bench was

The Four Conditions of Society: Work. Jean Bourdichon (1457-1521)

set a quartern measure of gin, a crust of bread, and a slice of cheese. Attracted by the odour of the latter dainty, a hungry cat had contrived to scratch open the paper in which it was wrapped, displaying the following words in large characters: – "THE HISTORY OF THE FOUR KINGS, OR CHILD'S BEST GUIDE TO THE GALLOWS." And, as if to make the moral more obvious, a dirty pack of cards was scattered, underneath, upon the sawdust. Near the door stood a pile of deal planks, behind which the carpenter ensconced himself in order to reconnoitre, unobserved, the proceedings of his idle apprentice.

"Standing on tiptoe, on a joint-stool, placed upon the bench, with his back to the door, and a clasp-knife in his hand, this youngster, instead of executing his appointed task, was occupied in carving his name upon a beam, overhead."

Sheppard goes from bad to worse, turning to thievery instead of carpentry after falling in with a bad crowd, and eventually is hanged for it (as was the real-life notorious criminal Jack Sheppard, on whom the novel was based). But the carpentry does come in handy; he's awfully good at navigating locked doors and windows, and can handily saw his way through an iron spike.

Woodworking also shows up in Herman Melville's *Moby Dick* (1851) – The Carpenter even gets his own chapter (107).

"The one grand stage where he enacted all his various parts so manifold, was his vice-bench; a long rude ponderous table furnished with several vices, of different sizes, and both of iron and of wood. At all times except when whales were alongside, this bench was securely lashed athwartships against the rear of the Try-works.

"A belaying pin is found too large to be easily inserted into its hole: the carpenter claps it into one of his ever-ready vices, and straightway files it smaller. A lost land-bird of strange plumage strays on board, and is made a captive: out of clean shaved rods of right-whale bone, and cross-beams of sperm whale ivory, the carpenter makes a pagoda-looking cage for it. An oarsman sprains his wrist: the carpenter concocts a soothing lotion. Stubb longed for vermillion stars to be painted upon the blade of his every oar; screwing each oar in his big vice of wood, the carpenter symmetrically supplies the constellation. A sailor takes a fancy to wear shark-bone ear-rings: the carpenter drills his ears. Another has the toothache: the carpenter out pincers, and clapping one hand upon his bench bids him be seated there; but the poor fellow unmanageably winces under the unconcluded operation; whirling round the handle of his wooden vice, the carpenter signs him to clap his jaw in that, if he would have him draw the tooth."[18]

He also builds a coffin for the ill Queequeg, who, after rallying from his deathhammock (as opposed to deathbed), uses it thereafter as a sea chest. And of course, the carpenter fashions Captain Ahab's whalebone peg leg.

In Gustav Flaubert's 1856 *Madame Bovary*, the tax collector, Monsieur Binet, finds solace in working at his lathe, "and amused himself by turning napkin rings, with which he filled up his house, with the jealousy of an artist and the egotism of a bourgeois."[19] The monotonous humming of the tool recurs throughout the novel, serving to drive Emma Bovary to distraction as she yearns to escape what she sees as the unbearable confines of her provincial life. In the end, she poisons herself to escape the debt she accrued while trying to escape her boredom – she'd have been better off taking up turning than gambling.

For my final woodworking reading recommendation, I'm going back – way back – to middle English poetry. "The Debate of the Carpenter's Tools" is an anonymous work that pits the workman's tools against one another in defending their master, and it's an excellent source for finding out what woodworking tools were used in the medieval period. I encourage you to cover the right side of the opposite page, and read the excerpts aloud, speaking the words phonetically – I'll bet you recognize the tools and the gist of the discussion:

Then seyd the Whetston,
"Thof my mayster thryft be gone,
I schall hym helpe within this yere
To gete hym twenti merke clere.
Hys axes schall I make full scharpe,
That thei may lyghtly do ther werke.
To make my master a ryche man
I schall asey if that I cane."

To hym than seyd the Adys,
And seyd, "Ye, syr, God gladys.
To speke of thryfft, it wyll not be,
Ne never I thinke that he schall thé.
For he wyll drynke more on a dey
Than thou cane lyghtly arne in twey;
Therfor thi tonge I rede thou hold
And speke no more no wordys so bold."

The Brode-Ax seyd withouten mysse;
He seyd, "The Pleyn my brother is;
We two schall clence and make full pleyn,
That no man schall us geynseyn,
And gete oure mayster in a yere
More sylver than a man may bere."

"Ye, ye," seyd the Twyvete,
"Thryft, I trow, be fro you sette.
To kepe my mayster in his pride,
In the contré ye canne not byde
Without ye stele and be thefys
And put meny men to greffys.
For he wyll drynke more in a houre
Than two men may gete in fowre.
When ye have wrought all that ye canne,
Yit schall he never be thryfty mane."

Therfor, wryghtys, take hede of this,
That ye may mend that is amysse,
And treuly that ye do your labore,
For that wyll be to your honour.[20]

(Then said the Whetstone,)
("Though my master's thrift be gone,)
(I shall him help within this year)
(To get him twenty marks clear.)
(His axes shall I make full sharp,)
(That they may lightly do their work.)
(To make my master a rich man)
(I shall assay, if that I can.")

(To him then said the Adze,)
(And said, "Yea, sir, God glads.)
(To speak of thrift, it will not be,)
(Nay, never I think that he shall see.)
(For he will drink more on a day)
(Then thou can lightly earn in three)
(Therefore, thy tongue I bid thou hold)
(And speak no more no words so bold.")

(The Broad Axe said without a miss;)
(He said, "The Plane my brother is;)
(We two shall cleanse and make full plane,)
(That no man shall us gainsay,)
(And get our master in a year)
(More silver than a man may bear.")

("Yea, yea," said the Twyvette,)
("Thrift, I trust, be from you set.)
(To keep my master in his pride,)
(In the country you cannot bide)
(Without, you steal and be a thief)
(And put many men to grief.)
(For he will drink more in an hour)
(Then two men may get in four.)
(When you have wrought all that you can,)
(Yet shall he never be a thrifty man.")

(Therefore, wrights, take heed of this,)
(That you may mend that is amiss,)
(And truly that you do your labor,)
(For that will be to your honor.)[21]

While there is no clear winner in the discussion (a common outcome in debate poems of the period), there is a clear loser: the carpenter. The message is this: Don't be a drunk (like this guy), and do good work. ◆

ENDNOTES

1. Daniel Defoe. *Robinson Crusoe*, Chapter 4. (Gutenberg.org.)
2. Ibid.
3. Ibid.
4. Ibid.
5. Ibid.
6. Ibid.
7. Daniel Defoe. *Robinson Crusoe*, Chapter 5 (Gutenberg.org.)
8. Ibid.
9. Daniel Defoe. *Robinson Crusoe*, Chapter 14. (Gutenberg.org.)
10. Daniel Defoe. *Robinson Crusoe*, Chapter 16. (Gutenberg.org.)
11. William Shakespeare. "A Midsummer Night's Dream." *The Norton Shakespeare* (New York: W.W. Norton, 1997)
12. George Eliot. *Adam Bede*, Chapter 12. (Gutenberg.org.)
13. George Eliot. *Adam Bede*, Chapter 1. (Gutenberg.org.)
14. Ibid.
15. George Eliot. *Adam Bede*, Chapter 4. (Gutenberg.org.)
16. George Eliot. *Adam Bede*, Chapter 15. (Gutenberg.org.)
17. William Harrison Ainsworth. *Jack Sheppard*. Book 2, Chapter 1. (Gutenberg.org.)
18. Herman Melville. *Moby Dick*. Chapter 107 (Gutenberg.org.)
19. Gustav Flaubert. *Madame Bovary*. Part 2, Chapter 1 (Gutenberg.org.)
20. http://d.lib.rochester.edu/teams/text/shuffelton-codex-ashmole-61-debate-of-the-carpenters-tools
21. Translation from Middle English by Michael Updegraff.

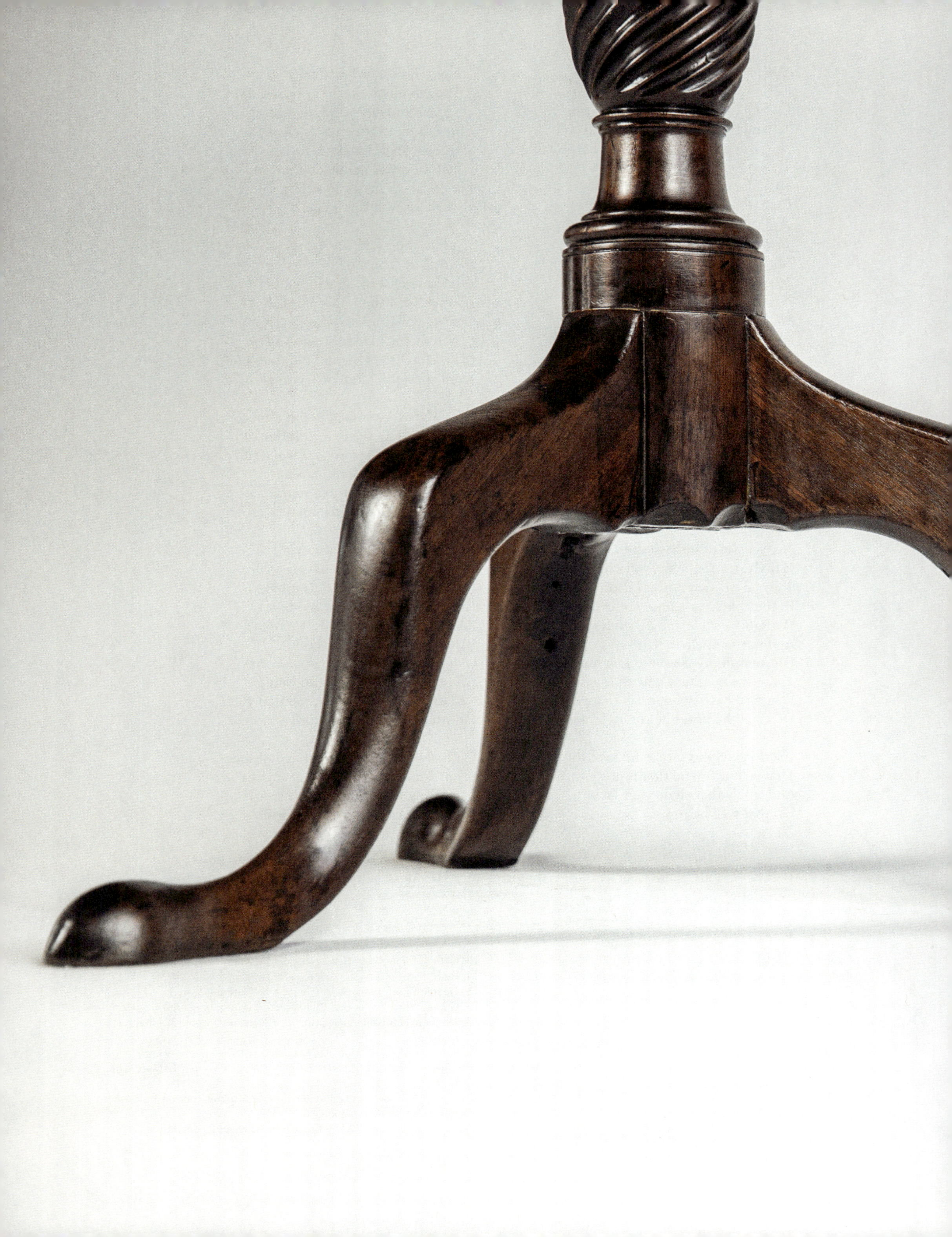

EXAMINATION *of an* 18th-century Mahogany Tea Table

This table recently received conservation treatment, during which the repair of a broken leg provided a unique opportunity to look inside the sliding dovetail joinery. Private Collection.

Wood:
Mahogany throughout

Dimensions:
Height: 27-3/4"
Diameter (top): 27"
Thickness (top): 13/16"

Leg Stock: 1-9/16"
At ankle: 1-5/16"
At toe: 1-9/16"

Cleats: 13/16"-thick material
1-1/8" tall, tapering at ends

Column:
Diameter at base: 3-1/4"
Sliding dovetails: 3-1/2" tall
Bottom of column to floor: 6-1/2"
Top of leg to floor: 9-15/16"

Block: 1-1/4" thick, 5-3/8" x 5-3/4"
Column tenons (x2) into block: 5/8" thick
Block tenons into cleats: 3/4" round

Tapered sliding dovetail

Iron spider bracket now missing,
screw holes visible under legs

Lathe center, overcut dovetails, rasp marks

Tapered sliding dovetail, undercut at base to ease assembly

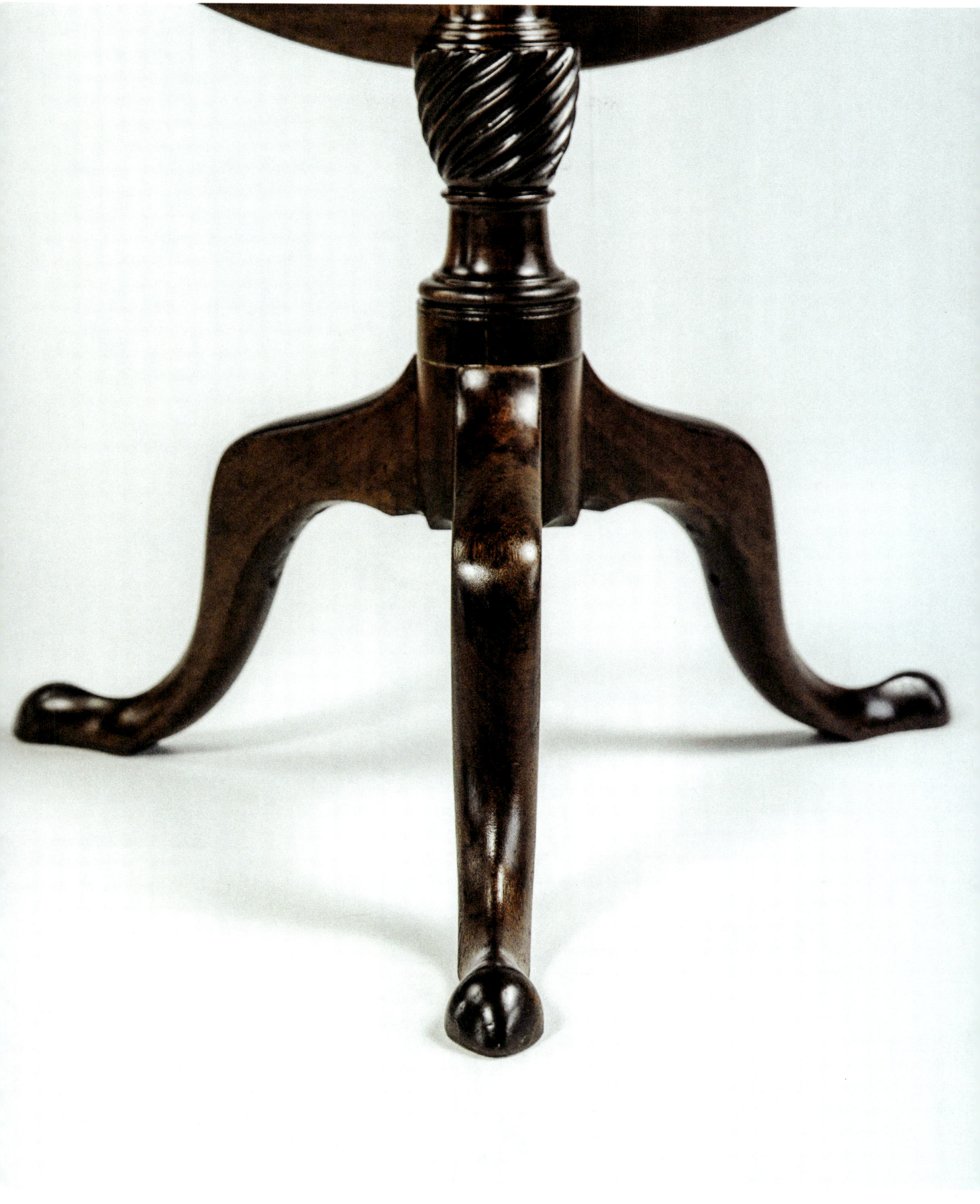

Turned column with spiral-fluted urn

(Diameters listed.)

— 3-1/4"

— 2"

— 2-1/2"

— 2-1/8"

— 2-5/16"

— 2-1/2"

— 3-1/8"

— 2"

— 2-9/16"

— 3-1/8"

— 2-1/4"

— 2"

— 3-1/4"

Tilt-top block. Top was through-fastened with screws at one time. Latch missing.

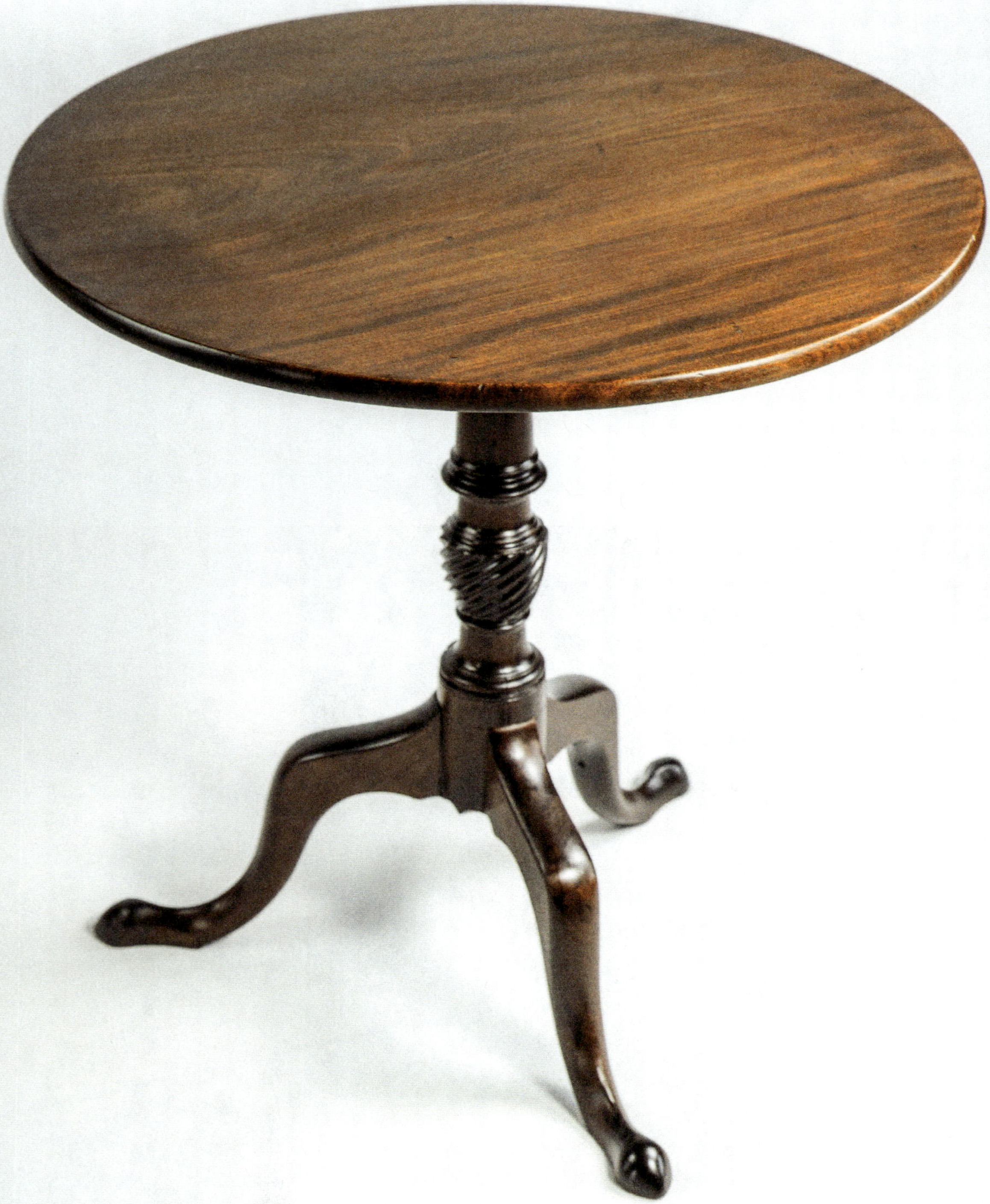

Four diamond patches on top (center) cover previous screw holes.

Photo: Bob Adelman

AN OVERWHELMING CALL

The Life & Work of Eric Sloane

Michael Updegraff

All images in this article used with kind permission from the Eric Sloane Estate.

"The craftsman of yesterday['s]...ways were honest and lasting and beautiful to an extent that is today deemed over and above requirements. How poor and dishonest and ugly and temporary are the results of so many modern workers whose constant aim is more to make the most money from their profession instead of producing the most honest and beautiful and lasting things. I feel that a good way of studying the conscience and personality of the anonymous pioneer American – so that I may emulate some of his ways – is by collecting and analyzing the tools with which he worked."

– Eric Sloane

Eric Sloane did not mince words. Thumb through a copy of one of his books and you might be struck not simply by the charming pen-and-ink drawings depicting early rural life or the elaborate catalogs of vernacular tools for working both soil and wood, but also by stern admonitions set forth regarding the direction that American society has taken in the last century. Eric Sloane's legacy is as complex as the man himself. To better understand that legacy we must seek to grasp just how powerful the call of yesteryear was in his life – a call whose thread can be traced to his earliest days.

Becoming Eric Sloane

In 1925, the troubled young American artist hit the road in search of a new start. Born Everard Jean Hinrichs, the son of German immigrants, he suffered a lengthy series of struggles and setbacks that led to his decision to head west and explore the country his family had adopted. Ostensibly borrowing the family's neglected Model T, Hinrichs fashioned counterfeit license plates and left all he knew in New York City. Trained in painting and lettering, and inspired by the boundless vistas of the Hudson River School movement of romantic landscape art, he planned to work his way across America as a freelance sign painter while learning the moods and history of the land.

Hinrichs' ancestry and ability to letter in

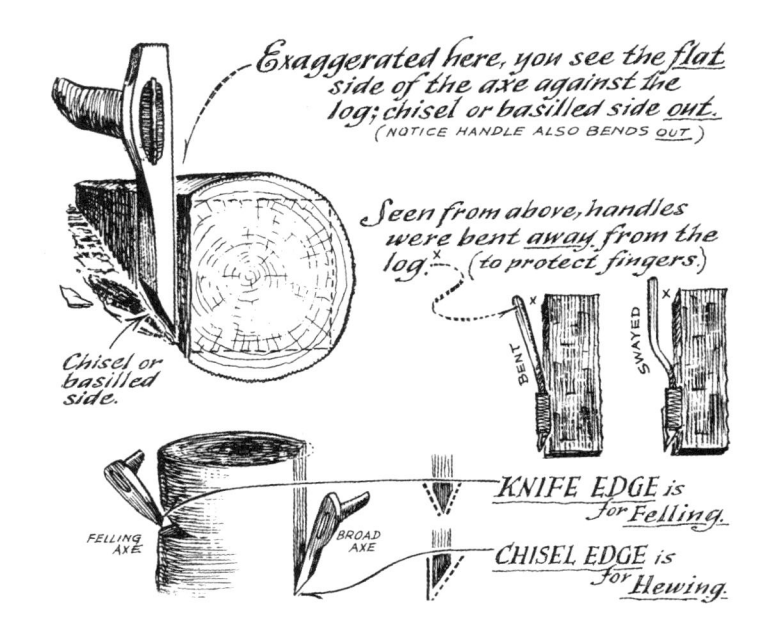

"October Colors" 19" x 33" Oil on Masonite.

Old German endeared him to the Amish of Lancaster, Pennsylvania, with whom he stayed and worked for some time. He was struck by the simple beauty of their well-crafted timber and stone barns, and discovered the traditional barn lore kept alive in those communities. Hinrichs here became acquainted with hand-tool woodworking, and the deep reverence that the Amish possess for the land, for faith, and for community – values that stuck with the young man all his life.

As the old Model T continued its westward journey into Ohio, Hinrichs decided to implement advice that an art school mentor had given him years earlier – adopting a pen name. This alias enabled a young artist to practice creative exploration without later being saddled to early, faltering works; he could simply move on from the name once skills and technique had been developed. Hinrichs borrowed and altered the last name of one of his early teachers, John Sloan, and Americanized his own first name (literally, by pulling the letters from the middle of the word "America") to create the persona that would become familiar to millions. Everard Hinrichs became Eric Sloane.

Signs and the Sky

From Mail Pouch Tobacco barns to store windows, from covered bridges to road signs, Eric Sloane found that he could secure all the sign-painting work he needed, and his artistic reputation began to precede him as he traveled. In exchange for lettering a barnstorming biplane, Sloane was given his first flight – an experience that profoundly impacted his career. He began to study the sky as his horizons broadened westward. That flight had given him new appreciation for the beauty and dynamic nature of clouds and storms, and by the time his old Ford chugged into New Mexico, Sloane's imagination was captured. He began trying to render the expansive views of the Western sky on Masonite sign boards, using his lettering paints to explore the beauty of clouds and earth. After drifting around the country for several more years, Sloane returned to New York City in 1933 to pursue his new passion.

Sloane's first "cloudscape," a painting of a towering thunderstorm, was purchased by legendary aviator Amelia Earhart. He began taking more frequent flights to study the sky and observe weather patterns. The technical aspects of clouds and weather fascinated him. He began studying the fledgling science of meteorology at MIT and was among the nation's first televised weathermen in 1939. His expertise in the field made him a frequently sought authority, and he was commissioned to write several books detailing weather phenomena for U.S. military pilots during World War II. That career hit a dead end, however, as Sloane found that his awe for the power of weather was snuffed out by dry mathematics. Firsthand study and observation were more valuable for his own understanding than classroom lectures, and he longed for more intimate knowledge than pressure charts and hourly reports allowed. Sloane remembered the close connection with weather and seasons that his Amish friends had demonstrated, and he began seeking new insight in old sources. Poring through early almanacs and farm diaries, he was astonished by their perceptiveness. "I found that the pioneer countryman was peculiarly aware of the sky, with an extraordinary knowledge of weather because his daily living so depended upon it," he wrote. Without the advantage of modern technology, the early farmer sensed the slightest change in wind and sky, and the cycles of his life moved with them. This was the connection for which Sloane was searching.

The Call of the Past

Inspired by the almanacs, Sloane began to research the lore and knowledge of the early American farmer. With his trademark brand of singular enthusiasm, he filled his living room with period journals and chronicles, and studied old letters and books. Sloane's art reflected the change; where previously a typical painting was composed of a cloudscape and perhaps a bit of horizon, the focus shifted downward to the bucolic scenes of early American farm life. He remembered the moment of transition: "My business with the sky was interrupted one day when I stood in the penetrating loneliness of an abandoned New England barn and felt the presence of the great American past. Just as a sudden accident can end a man's career, an instant mood can change the path of a well-chosen pursuit. It was a lifetime ago, but I recall that instant clearly, standing in the barn on hay that was strewn there over a century earlier but still perfumed the stillness. I remember how that quiet was broken by the faraway drone of an airplane, like background music to the contrast of yesterday and today. Perhaps that old barn was waiting for it to happen, because the communication was magic; I was confronted with an overwhelming call and I decided that the sky could wait." It wasn't the old building itself that captured Sloane – it was the understanding that some long-deceased soul, walking the same ground as he stood, had poured himself into this creation; he had labored, sweated, pondered, and prevailed here. The ramshackle barn was not just a quaint New England scene – it was a testament to the character of an ancestor. The "overwhelming call" of history had taken hold.

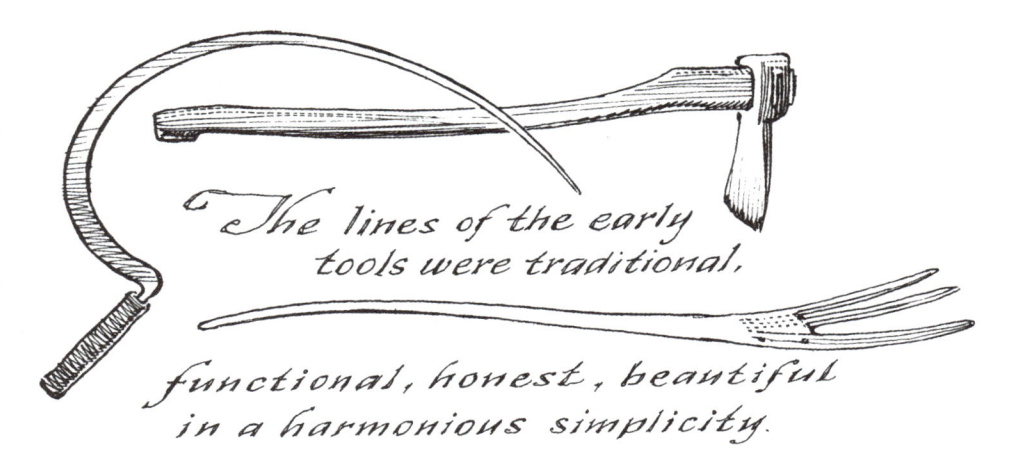

"The lines of the early tools were traditional, functional, honest, beautiful in a harmonious simplicity."

Once, while helping to dismantle another old barn, Sloane came across the imprint of a hand in the foundation plaster. He wrote of that experience, "Every line, callus, and scar was there, and as I placed my hand in the imprint to compare sizes, I had the strange feeling of someone from the past reaching down through the years to touch me." The almanacs, books, and material culture he was exploring pointed to an ancient humanity whose thoughts and ways were almost completely foreign to modern experience. Sloane began pondering some existential questions. In a chapter of *American Yesterday* (1956) titled "How Different was Great-grandfather?" he explored these contemplations. "We are supposed to be healthier, wealthier, and living in better times. Few of us would argue with that contention. But is the man at the wheel of today's automobile essentially the same man who drove a surrey a century ago? Is he the same kind of man merely wearing different clothes and doing different things, or has he actually undergone a physical and mental and spiritual change? If there is some change, no matter how small, it seems worthy of study. It could be one of the important observations of our time."

"The Green Door" 15-1/2" x 27"
Oil on Masonite.

Many of Sloane's books of this period, including *Our Vanishing Landscape*, *American Yesterday*, and *The Seasons of America Past*, are often classified as "Americana," a term he approached with caution because of its nostalgic connotations. Sloane distrusted the concept of nostalgia, saying, "I regard nostalgia as a kind of disease and I cringe when my [works] are referred to as nostalgic instead of poems of awareness, monuments to meaningful antiquity." He pushed against the widespread sentimentality he saw for things gone by simply by virtue of their being old. Instead, it was the recovery of the worthwhile attitudes and ways of the past that Sloane desired. Filled with rich pen-and-ink drawings to complement the text, his books were intended to unlock the moods of early rural life for his readers. He approached his anthropological studies with an artist's perspective, just as he had his meteorological studies years earlier.

Dry history books, replete with dates and names and events, contained little of the life Sloane found in original sources he collected. He felt the weight of real humanity behind diaries and notes, in barns and houses, and wished to convey as much of that humanity as he could. Of the typically modern view that life centuries ago must have been dreary and the people generally unhappy, Sloane countered, "See how carefully and beautifully people created things in those days. How aware these people were of the kinds of materials they worked with. How aware they were of the time in which they lived, everything is dated and signed. How richly awake they must have been to every moment of each day!" He felt that the good things of the past were not just the articles made (the material culture left behind) but "the manner in which people lived and the things that people thought." These were the things most worth preserving.

Tools: A Connection to the Past

Wandering abandoned farmsteads and rebuilding stone walls (a favorite hobby), Sloane made more discoveries: old tools, tucked away in the corner of a hayloft or hanging on some forgotten peg. He found a bog-iron gouge that had been long hidden in a stone fence and marveled at the durability of the tool to survive rust-free for centuries. In these tools, he found his deepest connection with the past.

"When we consider tools, we are dealing with human benefactors of the most primary sort. Tools increase and vary human power; they economize human time, and they convert raw substances into valuable and useful products. So when we muse on historic tools as symbols, we are always analyzing the romance of human progress." Sloane liked to quote Henry Ward Beecher in saying that "a tool is but the extension of a man's hand," and he began to regard the early tools he found this way – particularly user-made varieties. He did not find much of interest in the mass-produced implements of the post-Civil War period. Vernacular, shop-made tools bore real, physical memory of the hands that shaped and held them.

"For a long while I have collected early American wooden tools – those things that pioneer people fashioned at home. It seems that they put so much of themselves into these implements that just being with them is like being with the people who created them. Closing your hand around a worn wooden hammer handle is very much like reaching back into the years and feeling the very hand that wore it smooth."

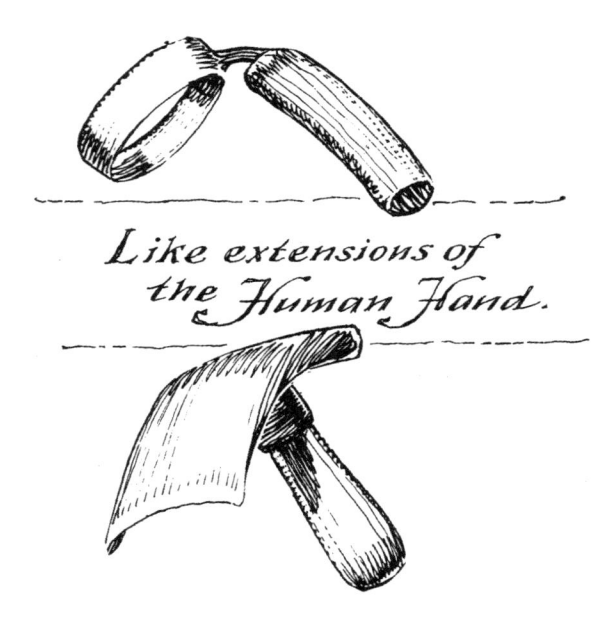

Sloane's 1964 book, *A Museum of Early American Tools*, is often credited with igniting the antique tool collecting renaissance that continues to this day. In it, he illustrates hundreds of forms of pre-industrial hand tools, demonstrating proper usage and sharing whimsical anecdotes. His philosophy of tools as the highest articulation of past culture, folk art in its purest form, is presented vividly. *A Reverence For Wood* (1965) continues in the same vein, focusing on the lore and historical usage of trees as a resource, and he connects points in his argument in a way that has been called "almost mystical." This near-mysticism and whimsy is a point of contention often raised by Sloane's detractors who prefer a textbook approach to recording history, and even go so far as to call some of his work fictional. However, Sloane intentionally steered away from the textbook approach, seeking instead to recall the past using words on a page the way he painted with oils – freely using artistic liberty. He thought of writing as "speaking on paper, emoting on paper, remembering on paper." Just as his beloved almanacs shared real knowledge by expressing fanciful rhymes and tales, Sloane wrote to convey information while achieving what he called "poetic sense." He believed that if his writing failed to transmit the feelings of awe and appreciation that he experienced in getting to know his forebears, he had done his readers a disservice.

The Virtue of the Vernacular

In his art and writing, Sloane focused almost exclusively on the rural, simple, and plain. In fact, so obviously and predictably absent are any mention of high-style forms of furniture or architecture that the snubbing seems to carry a deliberate message. It is no mystery that it was in the country, in the fields and woods, rather than the bustling city, where the artist found the heart of what he most admired about the pre-industrial craftsman. In one book, mention is made of a beautiful table produced by the Dominy Shop of rural East Hampton, New York. Sloane's purpose in introducing this table was to counter the modern perception of the crudity of tools and benches with the beauty that the Dominy craftsmen could produce. Even in discussing this fine piece of furniture, his emphasis remained on the skill and character of the period makers and on their simple tools, rather than the objects they made.

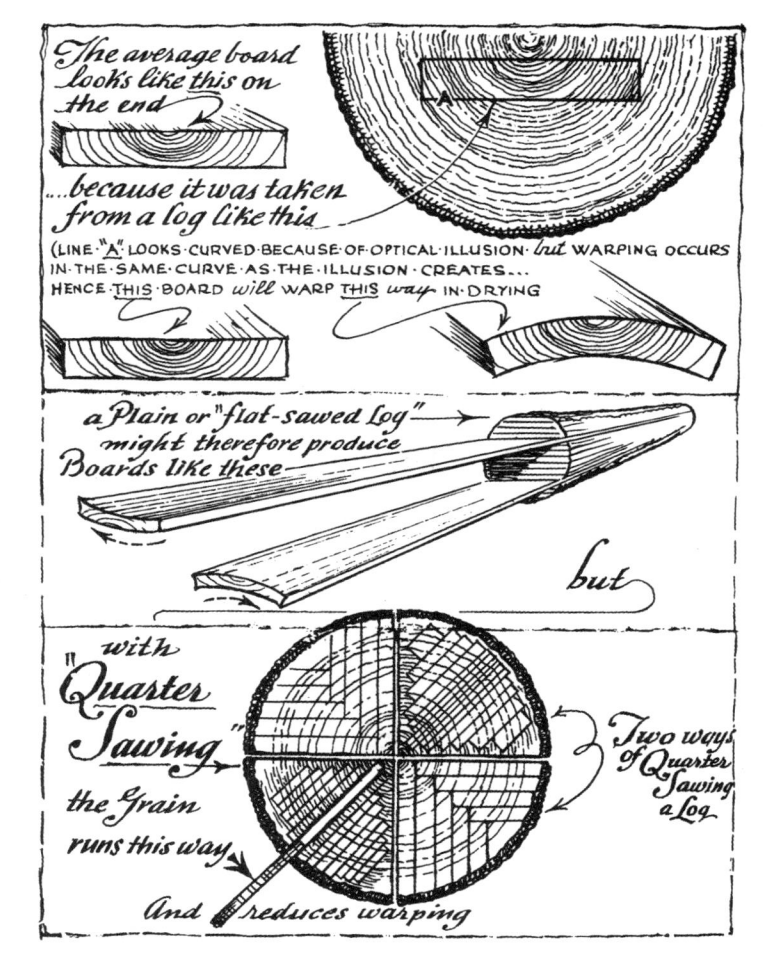

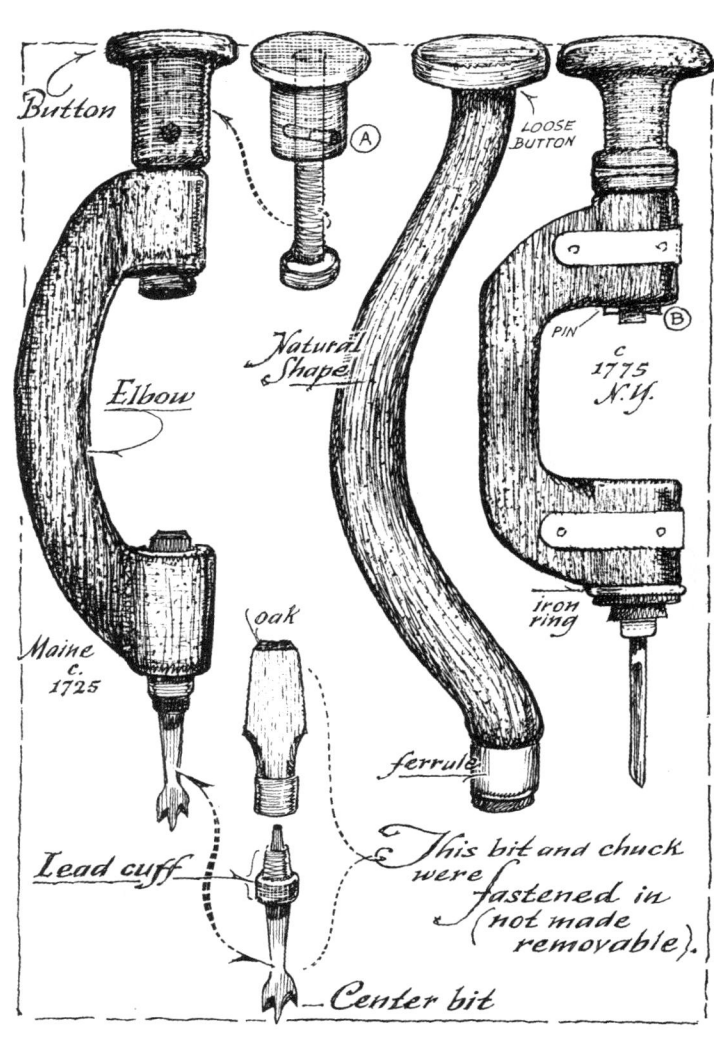

Legacy

In the late 1960s, Stanley Tool Works collaborated with Sloane to open the Sloane-Stanley Museum (now the Eric Sloane Museum) in Kent, Connecticut. The grounds feature the 1826 Kent Iron Furnace as well as the museum itself, which houses the entirety of Sloane's collection of early tools. The artist painstakingly placed each artifact on display and lettered every description. To date, nothing has been altered from his original vision. Sloane desired to tell a story with these implements, and the museum offers the sense of being inside one of his books.

The corpus of Sloane's life work is vast. He painted nearly every day, totaling some 15,000 works, with untold numbers beyond that destroyed by the artist because they fell short of what he sought to achieve. His largest painting, a mural roughly 60' x 75', graces the main hall of the National Air & Space Museum in Washington, D.C. The speed with which he worked was legendary, much like that of the craftsmen of old he admired. A story is told of a mural he had been commissioned to paint on the wall of a company headquarters. Believing that Sloane would be busy for the rest of the week with his task, the company executives left him in the morning, planning on checking in at the end of the day. Sloane finished, packed up, and was gone just after lunchtime.

He wrote and illustrated almost a book per year from the 1940s until his death in 1985. Like his painting, the skill and speed he showed in his pen-and-ink illustrations was astonishing. He spent untold hours signing books for admirers, and many of those signatures were accompanied by fanciful sketches he completed in seconds, often without lifting his pen from the paper.

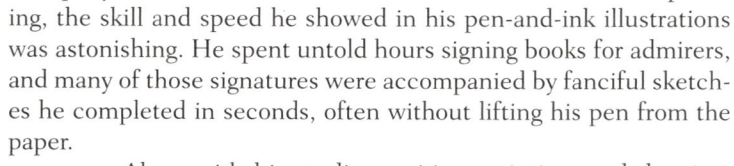

Along with his studies, writing, painting, and drawing, Sloane found time to restore more than 20 old homes and structures, as well as rebuilding miles of New England stone walls. But perhaps his greatest legacy is the awareness he has kindled for generations of readers about the value of remembering the ways of the past.

Sloane certainly viewed "progress" with some suspicion. He saw the advancement of technology and corresponding changes in basic human behavior as being dangerously near the point of spiraling out of control. He believed that the unchecked blitz of automated technology and of a throwaway society would increas-

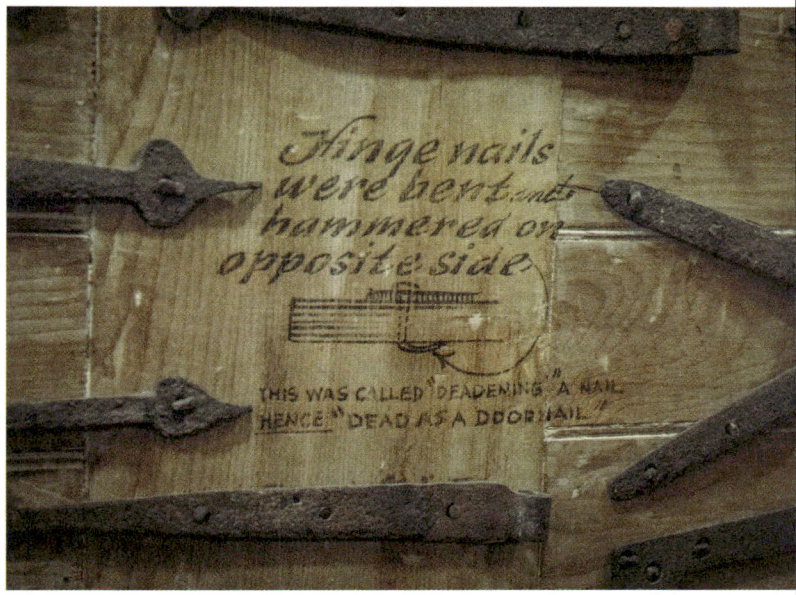

Hinge nails were bent and hammered on opposite side. This was called "deadening" a nail, hence "dead as a doornail."

The GRAND UNION
used by Washington during
the Revolution

APPLE-BUTTER PADDLES

Reverence for Wood

GRAIN SHOVELS

APPLE SHOVEL

in The Cooperage trade there was

the **Wet Cooper** who made containers for liquids from White oak and Ash..
— Liquids, Sap carriers, Tubs and Piggins

the **Dry Cooper** or "Slack cooper" used maple, oak, ash, hickory, chestnut, to make containers for... Sugar... Flour... Cakes, Grain

the **White Cooper** used Pine, birch, maple, ash
— Nests of Boxes, Baskets, Pails, Bowls, Boxes etc.

ingly detach us from our surroundings, making us "less aware, always more under the influence of powers beyond our comprehension." He was a pragmatist when it came to technology, and readily admitted the infeasibility of taking a societal U-turn back to simpler times, but he warned that our increased dependence on an industrial system for our needs, rather than the skill of our own hands and sweat of our brow, would have consequences. "We must expect some starvation of self-expression," he wrote. "There is a moral emptiness that comes when we are deprived of the satisfaction of doing things for ourselves."

Sloane was convinced that the best way to learn from history was to maintain a steady focus on the good that existed in the past, on traits and works that were admirable and worthy of emulation. While recognizing that mistakes and evils are perpetuated in every age, Sloane preferred the optimist's perspective that the glass of history is half full. He believed that the way forward is to rediscover those parts of the past that can encourage us to hold fast to purpose, to community, to awareness. Even as he wrote, "Indeed, there are ugly things in all ages which should be discarded and forgotten," he chose to cling to the good in those who came before.

At times one gets the sense, especially in reading his later books, that Sloane felt he was fighting a losing battle. There is a sadness and a resignation present in these that certain things have been lost that cannot be regained, ways forgotten that will not be remembered. His epitaph, carved into the weathered boulder by which he is buried, reflects this sentiment with the words, "God Knows I Tried." Sloane sought for most of his adult life to make a connection across the ages, to better know himself by knowing those in whose footsteps he walked. He could hear their voices in the things they made, the words they wrote, and the tools they used – and in those same ways, by the same means, we can today hear the voice of Eric Sloane among them. ◆

ACKNOWLEDGMENTS

I am grateful to the Eric Sloane Museum and the Friends of the Eric Sloane Museum for providing access to the Sloane collection and assistance for my research.

REFERENCES

Mauch, James W. *Aware: A Retrospective of the Life and Work of Eric Sloane*. Laurys Station, Pa: Garrigues House, 2000.
Sloane, Eric. *A Museum of Early American Tools*. New York: Funk & Wagnalls, 1964.
———. *A Reverence for Wood*. New York: Funk & Wagnalls, 1965.
———. *Diary of an Early American Boy*. New York: Random House, 1965.
———. *Eric Sloane's America*. New York: Promontory Press, 1982.
———. *The Spirits of '76*. New York: Walker And Company, 1973.

Tool House in *Berks County Pennsylvania*

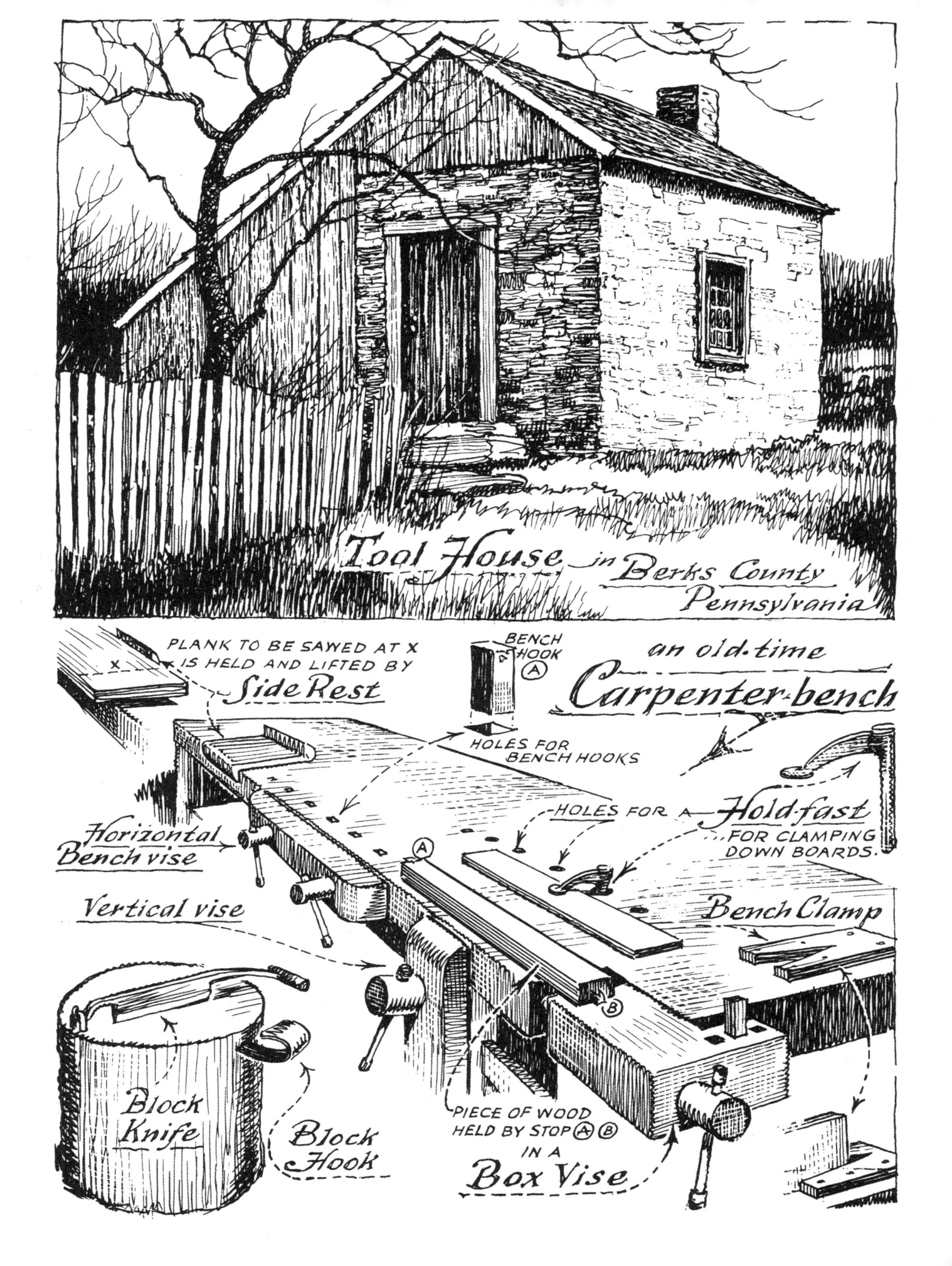

an old-time *Carpenter-bench*

PLANK TO BE SAWED AT X IS HELD AND LIFTED BY *Side Rest*

Bench Hook Ⓐ

HOLES FOR BENCH HOOKS

HOLES FOR A *Hold-fast* FOR CLAMPING DOWN BOARDS.

Horizontal Bench vise

Bench Clamp

Vertical vise

Block Knife

Block Hook

PIECE OF WOOD HELD BY STOP Ⓐ Ⓑ IN A *Box Vise*

"Finding an ancient tool in a stone fence or in a dark corner of some decaying barn is receiving a symbol from another world. ... When you hold an early implement, when you close your hand over the worn wooden handle, you know exactly how it felt to the craftsman whose hand had smoothed it to its rich patina. ... In that moment you are near to another being in another life, and you are that much richer."

– Eric Sloane

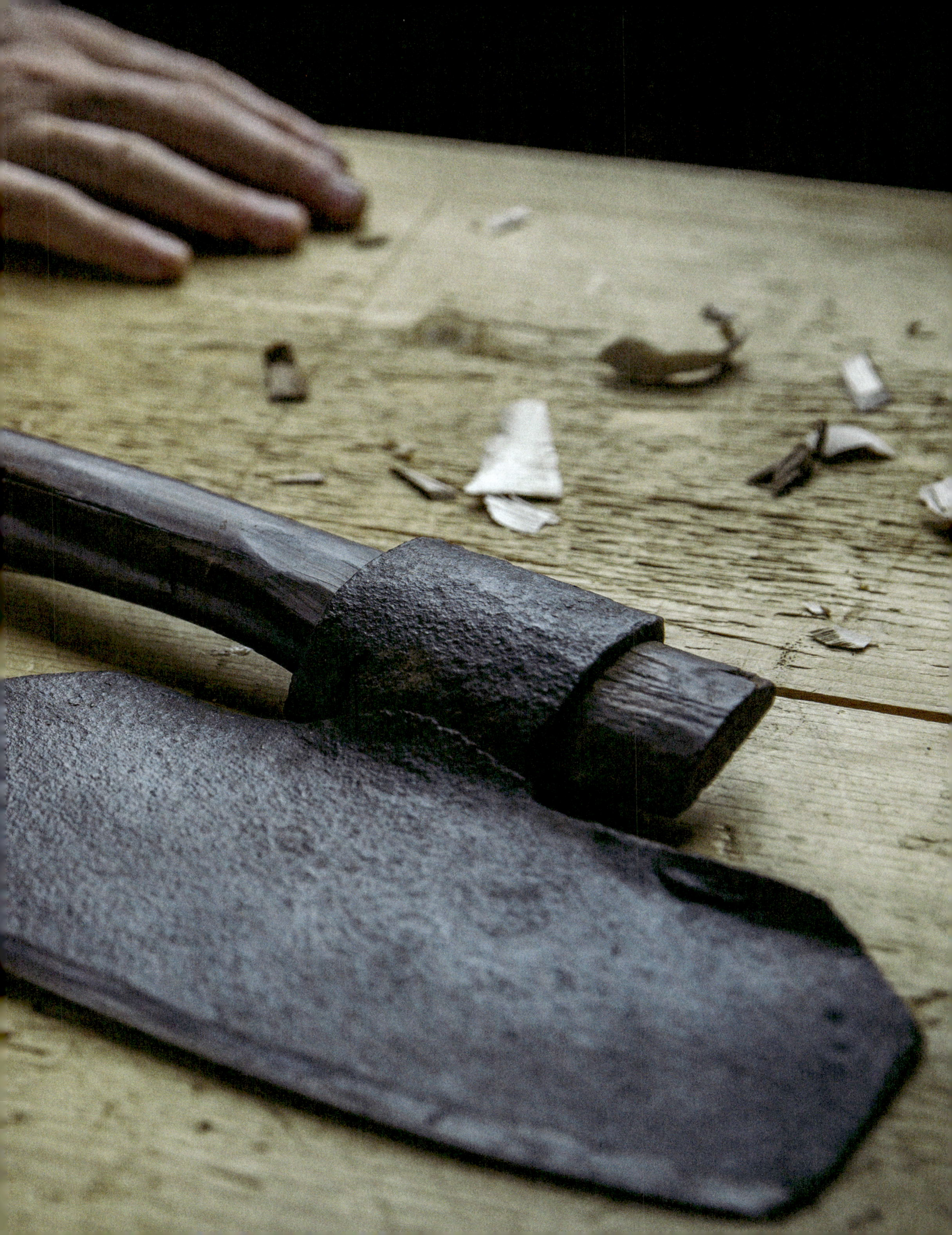

In Tight Quarters

A Conversation
with Spencer Nelson
About Apartment Woodworking

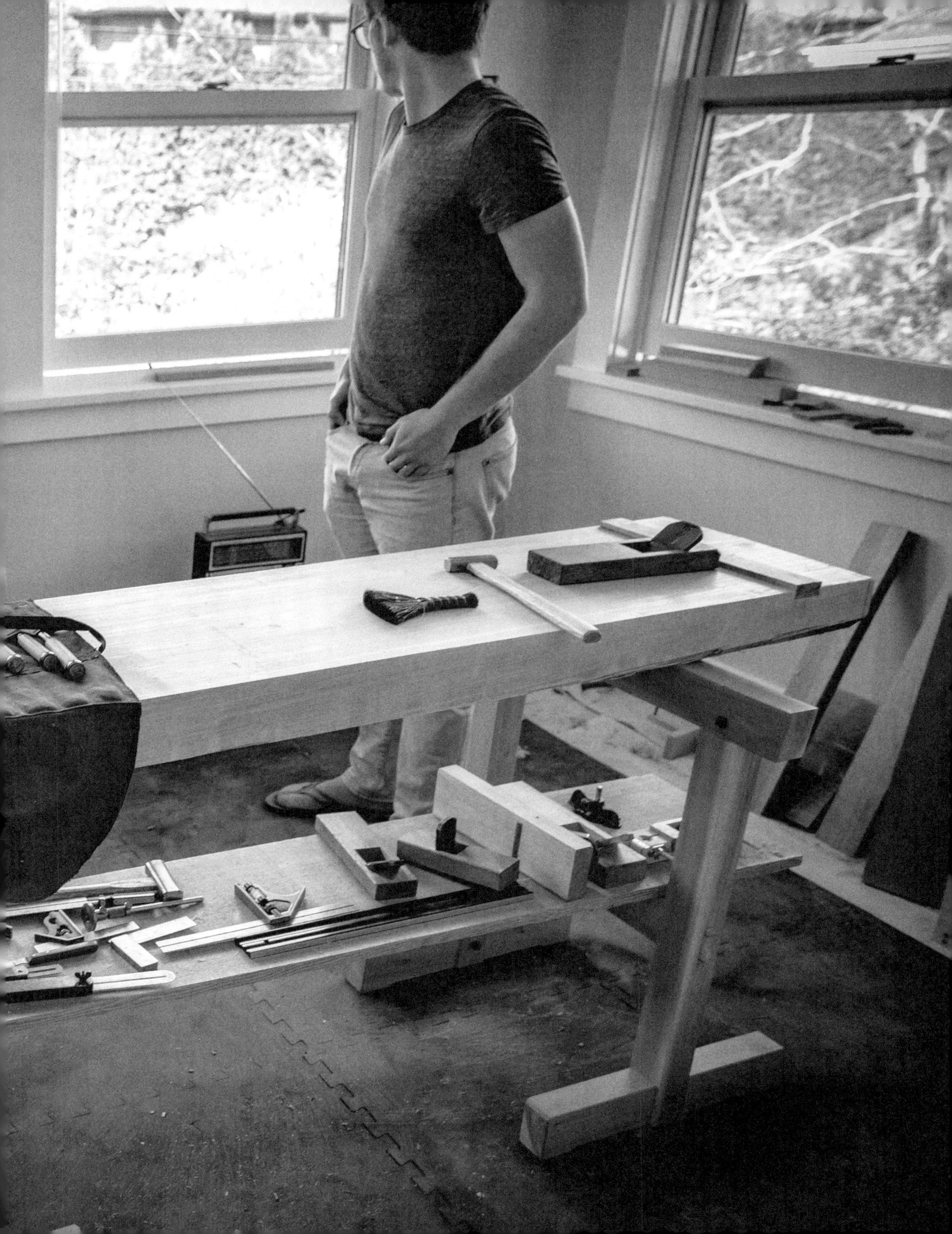

M&T: How long have you been working wood? How did you get started in it?

SN: Not that long, maybe three years or so. It started out of the restlessness I felt doing abstract stuff all the time at my day job. I'm a computer programmer so I work on really abstract backend systems, things very distant from human beings, from anything physical. I'd felt this craving building up to do things in the real world. At that time, I got really into sourdough bread baking. I quickly became obsessed and was making two loaves of bread every day. I had a starter to keep alive, cultivate, and feed. That started awakening this part of me that wanted to be more in touch with the physical world and the people around me. Woodworking became a way to satisfy that need. I went out to a community workshop called Makeville Studios in Brooklyn, New York, and took a "beginnings of woodworking" kind of class. It resonated with me right away and felt really good – this was the therapy I was after.

I began going to Makeville after work just to do something with my hands. I came back feeling great every time. Before long, I started going to a maker space about a mile and a half away from my house so that I could have my own bench space. Because I didn't have a car (in Brooklyn, who does?), I had to backpack all my wood a mile and a half to the maker space to work for two hours before hauling it all back in my backpack. It was difficult and I got tired of doing that pretty quickly so I decided to start working at home.

Because I couldn't have machinery in a small Brooklyn apartment, I started working with hand tools. I quickly realized I needed to learn to work efficiently with hand tools because I was spending forever dimensioning stock. I started taking classes from Yann Giguère at Mokuchi Studio. Yann works in the Japanese tradition and has definitely steered my direction in woodworking. It's funny to think about, but I ended up at Japanese hand-tool woodworking out of the constraints of working in an apartment.

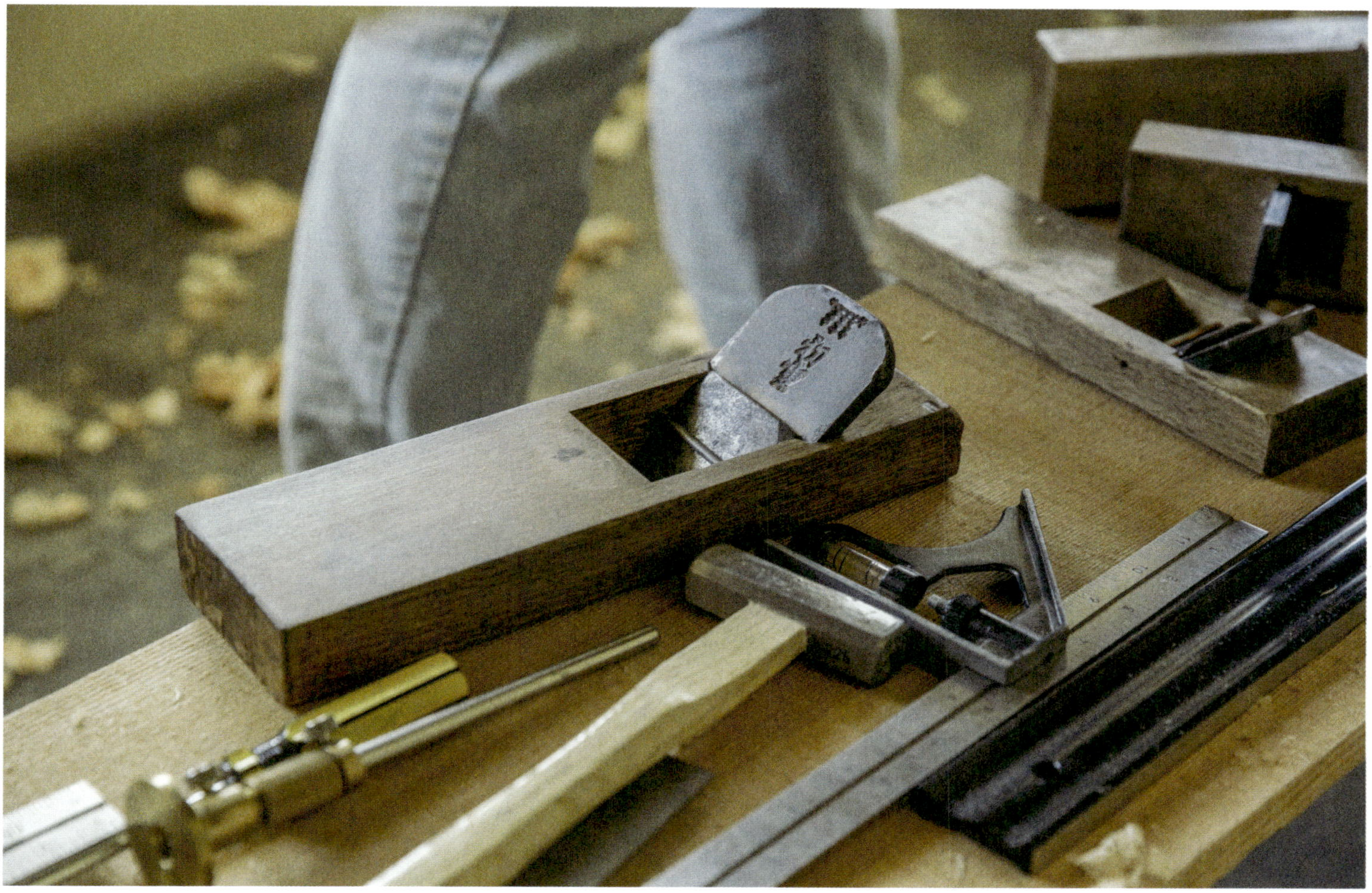

M&T: What was it like transitioning from the maker space into your own apartment workshop?

SN: While working in a shared space was interesting, I didn't feel a huge of amount of camaraderie that you might expect in a space like that. It might be that I felt too novice to be stepping into a space with lots of people doing serious production work, but, honestly, it just didn't really vibe with what I was getting out of woodworking. I remember one guy standing at the table saw all day making 60 cutting boards. I wanted to have a more intense focus on creating nice little things for friends.

At the same time, I had this dream of incorporating woodworking into my workday of programming at home. I envisioned being able to walk away from frustrating moments programming to sharpen chisels or resaw another board. Having a bench close by is important for that. I guess you could say that I set up shop at home out of a desire to escape from my computer.

M&T: Could you describe your workshop situation in the Brooklyn apartment?

SN: Sure. We were in a four-story, 12-unit, brick apartment building in Gowanus. We were on the third floor with neighbors above us, below us, and to one side. With neighbors so close, noise was the first consideration while thinking about how I was going to work. The second was figuring out how I could utilize the space. Our apartment was a long railroad-style apartment with a kitchen on one end, one big room in the middle, and a bedroom opposite – all the rooms connected in a long line. I had my workbench in the transition between the kitchen and the living room. It was a space of about 4-1/2' x 4-1/2'. I used a butcherblock baker's table as my workbench. I kept all my tools on the wall on shelves and had wood stacked along the wall lying flat.

The bench was about 24" deep and about 36" long. And it's a little high – something like 36". Honestly, though, it's amazing how much you can do on a really small surface. On the internet, you see lots of people saying, "If you're going to have a workbench, you need one that's at least 9' long and it's got to be a good 40" deep." And I thought, "Oh, man! That is my entire apartment."

Turns out it's not true. I was able to make some pretty big things in tight quarters. I made a record cabinet that's 4-1/2' long. One time, when I wanted to plane the top of a large coffee table I was making, I set the top on a few stools in front of the refrigerator and butted the end against the refrigerator. The fridge made a great planing stop. You can make a lot of stuff by navigating the space cleverly.

M&T: Where did you get your lumber and how did you process the rough stock?

SN: I got lumber from a lumberyard in the Bronx called Rosenzweig's and hauled wood home in a rental truck. I cut and ripped the stock with a handsaw and planed it to thickness with handplanes. I would estimate that I spent 60 to 70 percent of my time of any project on that part. It was really time-consuming but I got used to doing it. Yann taught me that it's good to learn to work without machines because I could learn a lot more about the shape of wood and how it responds than if I just fed it through a planer.

At the same time, though, when I had big projects that had a lot of ripping, I crosscut my stock to length and hauled it in the backpack to the maker space. I used the band saw for 45 minutes to do the ripping that would have taken me a week.

M&T: How is apartment woodworking unique? What special considerations need to be made and how did you navigate those constraints?

SN: You have to think about the time you work and so you end up planning the project around that. Chopping mortises is really loud so I tried to chop mortises between 10 a.m and 7 p.m. In the heart of the day nobody would've complained but I put foam mats under the workbench to try to deaden the noise anyway. It made the bench a bit squishy but you do what you've got to do. In addition to foam mats, hanging cloth in the area makes a big difference – carpets and cloth wall coverings really absorb noise. That said, there are a lot of hand-tool operations that don't make much noise – sawing is not that loud, really, unless you're sawing big boards across sawhorses. It's mostly about being attentive to the time of day and doing what you can to dampen the noise.

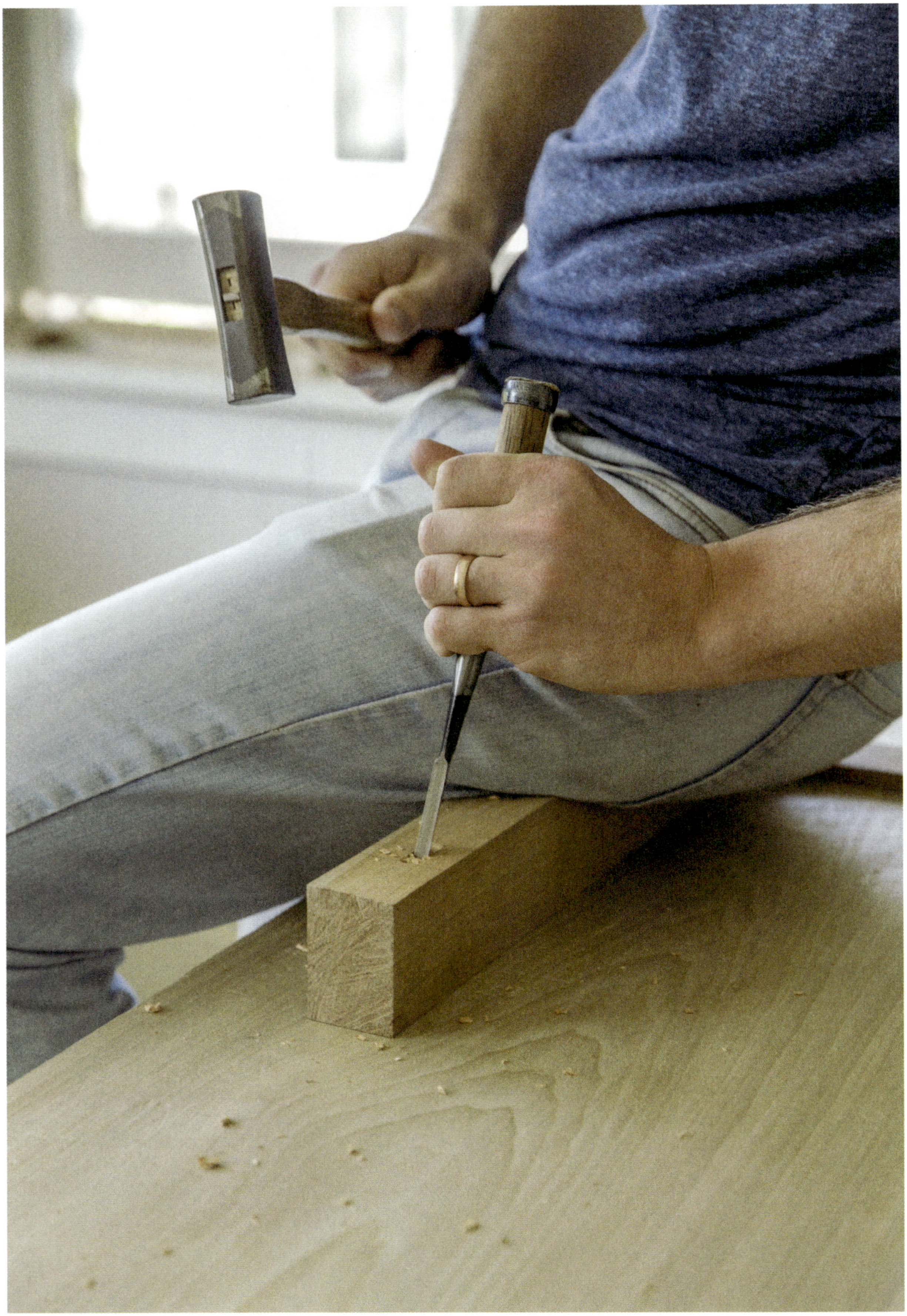

M&T: Did you have any situations in which your neighbors knocked on your door to complain about noise?

SN: Astonishingly, no. Not even once, and I don't know how because we had a lot of neighbors. I am still surprised that the neighbors below never complained but I guess it's less loud that you think. When you're standing right next to the hammer hitting the chisel, then it sounds really, really loud, but maybe a floor away it's not as bad.

I think if I had a day job out of the house and I was at the bench in the evenings, I would have talked to my neighbors first. I would open a dialogue where I could say, "I'm planning on doing some woodworking from 7 to 9 on these nights. Is that OK with you? Let me know if it's noisy." That would probably be the way I would go about it if I were working in the evenings.

M&T: How did you deal with the mess of working in a living space?

SN: Honestly, dust and plane shavings got everywhere. I'm lucky to have an awesome wife, who's OK with this, partly because she does spoon carving herself. We both made a huge mess and, at times, that stuff really took over. We didn't necessarily have a great strategy for dealing with it.

Being on top of cleaning before it gets out of control seemed to be the key. Wearing socks around plane shavings was one of the primary causes of their being transported to the rest of the house. Wearing shoes while working makes a big difference, even if you don't wear those shoes anywhere else in the house. But in reality we had plane shavings on the rugs, in the bathroom, and in our clothes.

Sanding with power tools makes a huge amount of dust. But that wasn't what I was doing. Using planes to smooth surfaces avoids that.

M&T: Definitely. How much setup and breakdown did you have between work sessions? Was your bench set up all the time or did you have to put everything away then take it all back out to work again?

SN: The bench was pretty much ready to go all the time but it was out of the way of normal life. When you're just starting out you just don't have that many tools to put away. I worked with exactly one saw, two planes, and four chisels for about a year and a half. With a minimal tool kit, it's not hard to clean up after each session. It was only when I was gluing up completed furniture that things sprawled out and took up a lot of space, but obviously that's not a huge amount of the overall process.

M&T: Can you tell us a little bit more about the workbench you were using?

SN: It's actually a stand for making bread on – a huge butcherblock on legs. It's pretty nice for bread baking but definitely not designed to be a workbench. It racks like crazy as you like plane across the top so I tried to reinforce it several times, but it never really worked. Honestly, when I was working, I didn't notice it that much. Maybe I didn't know any better but it never really bothered me.

I installed a tapered dovetail key planing stop. It's nothing fancy but it's really useful for doing just about any work because it's low profile and I can hold stock against it. I use this kind of stop for everything from planing boards to sawing tenons. It's simple and really effective. For anything long that I needed to hang over the edge, I removed the stop with a single hammer whack.

M&T: You've since moved to Seattle. Tell me about the space you work in now.

SN: Because of family connections, Seattle has always been an inevitable destination for my wife and me. Right now we're renting a house owned by a friend and my shop is in one of the bedrooms. The room is somewhere around 12' x 14'. I set woodworking aside for the first three months of living here because I was nervous about causing damage to the house. Pretty soon, though, I felt the urge to do manual work rising up again. I picked a room in the house and laid a canvas drop cloth with foam tiles on top of that. Because this is a nice, new floor, I wanted to avoid scratches from wood chips underfoot.

It's funny but, compared to my last apartment, this new shop space feels gigantic to me. I have a lot of room for storing wood right next to me, which is great. I get to have my tools all over the place and I have a 6'-long workbench. I genuinely don't know whether this would be considered a reasonably big workshop, but for me it feels huge. It almost feels like there's a lot of wasted space but I'm not going to complain.

This new bench is inspired by Yann's. It's basically a pair of sawhorses with a 4"-thick piece of poplar on top, not attached in any way. It's really heavy so it doesn't usually move without a tremendous amount of force. If it does, I clamp it in place. I didn't fasten the top because I occasionally want to move it so I can use the sawhorses as sawhorses. Underneath, I have a rough Douglas fir shelf stretching between the horses that I use for tool storage.

I think the best part of this new arrangement is really just having natural light here, which I didn't have in New York. Back there, I'd briefly get a little raking light in the kitchen but it's New York – there are tall buildings all over the place. So this is a real change.

M&T: What would you say to encourage emerging woodworkers who doubt they can do serious work in their apartments?

SN: The first thing is that if you have any impulse to do it, you should just go do it. And you should start now. I deeply regret not having started earlier. Not because I would have developed more skills by now, but because I wasted a lot of time doing other things when I could have been happier doing this. Woodworking is truly as fun as it sounds.

Another thing to keep in mind is that if you scale your projects down a bit, just about anything is doable in a small space. If you're making small boxes or stools, none of the parts are much longer than a couple feet. That is totally manageable on a small desk or kitchen counter. With one saw, two chisels, and one block plane, you can really do an astonishing amount of work. That's what I did and it really worked. You'll have to embrace the fact that it's going to take awhile to make things under those settings, but to me, that was almost an advantage because that meant I got plenty of enjoyment out of it.

I believe you'll never know how much you'll like something until you just jump up and do it. It's true that the basic set of woodworking tools can be intimidatingly expensive. It seems many woodworkers are used to staggeringly expensive purchases, and they don't even recognize a saw and two chisels and a jack plane is going to run you at minimum $150-200. That's actually a huge amount for some people to just take a lark on this hobby.

M&T: What's the greatest lesson you've learned through this experience?

SN: Taking care of the tools to keep them in top condition. If you don't do that, everything else suffers. The maker space I was a part of had a few hand tools but they were poorly cared for. Even though they took pretty good care of their machine tools, their handplanes just mangled every board they touched. It was then that I realized how dull they were. I understand why they didn't maintain them, because they get rough use from lots of people and sharpening is nobody's favorite part.

But I cannot express how important sharpening is. It was a breakthrough in my work the day I realized it's not as if you are busy working wood at the bench then you have to stop doing the "real part" to go do some sharpening. Sharpening is the real part – it's an important aspect of working wood.

So I have focused on getting good at sharpening and it might be the thing I spend the most time on. It's something to start learning early and not to be afraid of. Even if you ruin a few edges before you develop the feel, it really pays off to learn this. If you're doing hand-tool woodworking, sharpening is really important. It's at the top of the list of the skills to develop because it's the skill that enables everything else you do. ◆

This article is adapted from Joshua Klein's new book, *Hands Employed Aright: The Furniture Making of Jonathan Fisher (1768-1847)* (Lost Art Press, 2018), which is a look at the work and life of a rural pre-industrial cabinet and chairmaker through his surviving tools, furniture, and journal entries. The book is available for purchase at www.mortiseandtenonmag.com.

Images used with permission of either Jonathan Fisher Memorial or Farnsworth Art Museum are noted with JFM or FM, respectively.

Hand in Hand
with Jonathan Fisher
Interacting with the Legacy of a Rural Artisan

Joshua A. Klein

My greatest mentor died almost 200 years ago. When I began researching in 2013 what is very likely the most complete surviving record of a pre-industrial American furniture maker, I had no idea how profoundly it would affect my own life's work. To start, the breadth of surviving material from Jonathan Fisher's (1768-1847) hand is overwhelming. Unlike most furniture research that relies on half-erased pencil inscriptions, period inventory books, and a comparison of construction techniques, this look into Fisher's legacy has been a matter of sifting through a massive collection of surviving furniture, tools, and documents. Not only is his house still standing and filled with furniture he made, but with the tools he used to make it, along with 35 years of daily journal records and personal letters that live in the archives of the Jonathan Fisher Memorial and the Farnsworth Art Museum. This unique combination of surviving tools, furniture, and journals gives us an unparalleled opportunity to peer into the life and work of a pre-industrial craftsman.

These five years lying on my back under furniture to examine tool marks have profoundly affected my perspective on historic craftsmanship. Fisher was a pragmatic artisan but he was one who delighted in the work of his hands. His work has a humble grace that is akin to that of the Shakers but it's the unique merger of conservative New England restraint with Fisher's own artistic proclivity that make this a compelling study.

It has been my goal to unearth everything I can about what this man did and what made him tick in order to pass his story on to 21st-century woodworkers. There are so many lessons to learn from those who have gone before us; when such a rare and clear window into their work emerges, we would do well to take heed.

JFM

Fisher's Life

As a child, Fisher spent much of his time doing farm labor and becoming "expert" with the axe. But this practice in hard labor went in hand with a strong desire for a liberal education. Fisher recalled, "Between the years of 10 and 15 of my age I began to exhibit some traces of a mechanical genius" and he considered alternative careers, "first to go to the blacksmith's trade, then to the cabinetmaker's and finally to the clockmaker's trade. In either of the last two mentioned I might no doubt have succeeded, but God had other employment for me."

At the encouragement of his mother, he determined to pursue his studies in preparation for a college education. Even as his childhood studies were "pleasant" and learned "with considerable ease," he noted how "many intervals were stolen" in reading, geometry, and "some mechanical employ." This merger of rigorous mental exercise with handcraft would come to typify the remainder of his life.

Fisher attended Harvard College and

eventually accepted a call to minister to the frontier town of Blue Hill in the District of Maine – a ministry in which he faithfully served for 41 years. As welcome a vacation spot as Midcoast Maine is today, in the first half of the 19th century it was inhospitable frontier wilderness. Between the notoriously recalcitrant populace and the lack of resources, the isolated frontier was a daunting mission. Kevin Murphy described Blue Hill in the 1790s as "a clutch of rude dwellings surrounded by some rickety tidal mills."[1] But Fisher felt a Divine call to serve in this frontier setting – the "infant part of the country" – because "it [was] difficult for them to find a sufficient number of candidates, who [were] willing even to come and preach among them, and much less to settle."[2] As one Blue Hill man said, "We are so as it wore out of the wourld that we don't hardly know wether we do rite or rong but we mean to do as well as we can."[3]

Fisher's most active furniture-making years were between 1796 (when he settled in Blue Hill) and 1820 (when he paid off all his home- and farm-building debt), and he was a model of hard work and ingenuity. The furniture he made was one of the many ways he supplemented his modest ministerial salary to build a comfortable life in the frontier. Between carpentry, surveying, hat making, book writing, painting, and much more, Fisher beautified the world around him to provide for his family.

One of the most astonishing aspects of this story is that from 1790 to 1835, Fisher recorded his daily activities, including where he went, what work he accomplished, and occasionally his thoughts and observations of the day's events. The journal entries are significant for their commonness. Everyday events were faithfully documented. Weather records, ministerial visits, books read, as well as his farm and shop work are all recorded in comprehensive mundanity.

Despite the volume of daily entries, the task of excavating a coherent narrative from the journals could only be accomplished alongside the surviving objects because, as consistent as they are, the lack of detail can at times be frustrating to insatiable researchers.

"January 1807…

28. Warm and rainy. Worked on picture frame 1/4 day = 9. Turned chair rounds.
29. Turned chair rounds and posts. Ground tools, etc.
30. Finished ready for painting a little chair. P.M. went to Mr. Nicholas Holt and wife. Stopped in the evening at Mr. Phineas Osgood's.
31. Wrote a sermon."

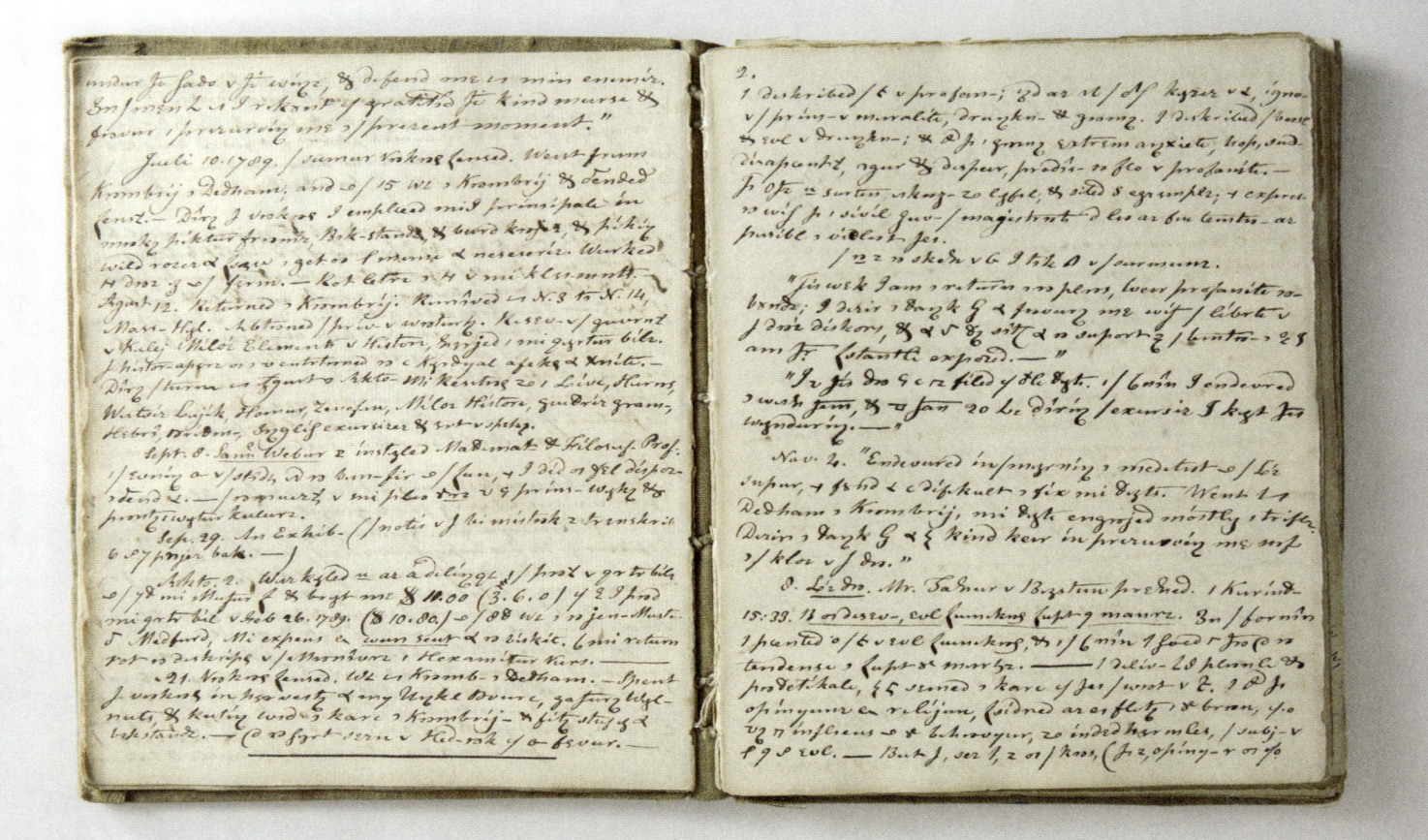

Rarely, there are projects that merited more particular attention, such as a chest of drawers Fisher worked on in December 1807:

10th: "…P.M. primed inside of sleigh and chest of drawers for Hannah Parker."
17th: "A.M. put locks and hinges on Hannah Parker's chest of drawers. P.M. painted it a second time and painted knapsack and inside of sleigh.."
18th: "Painted Hannah Parker's chest…"
29th: "Put trimmings on Hannah Parker's chest and carried it home."
30th: "Received of Hannah Parker for painting chest of drawers, etc. $1"

Understanding Fisher's Context

Fisher's life was far from easy. He regularly dealt with migraine headaches, stomach pains, diarrhea, and serious injuries from manual labor. Despite these trials, he resigned himself under the hand of Providence. Accounts such as that of August 28th, 1818, are common: "Came on for Bluehill exercised with pain in my side, back and bowels and with diarrhoea. Called at Phin. Osgood's, Jr. Reached home 10 P.M. Took sop pills and mullein tea. Found the family well, except Josiah, wounded by an ax. Have reason to bless God that we are all yet spared in life, that we have so many comforts indulged us."

Even in the midst of debilitating physical pain, Fisher carried on with the work at hand. On March 17, 1826, his journal reads, "High N.W. scattering clouds, cold. From 9 A.M. 'till about 5 P.M. exercised with earache, some of the time severely. Tried first camphor on wool, then hot tobacco smoke, then had several drops of West Indian Rum dropped

FM

FM

in. This in the first trial gave a little relief; in the second removed the severity of the pain. At intervals through the day planed out stuff for a common ruler, a pair of parallel rulers, and modern dividers, finished the latter. A part of the time walked the room in great pain. It is easy to bear pain when we do not feel it, but when it is acute, then to bear it with patience is something." Fisher was a resilient man.

The overwhelming body of artifacts now in the collections of the Jonathan Fisher House and the Farnsworth Art Museum unlock the story of this previously unstudied furniture maker. Examining in person the economy of construction in his use of rough-sawn and completely unplaned material for backboards partially explains the speed with which he made his furniture. What you don't see in the journals, however, is Fisher's penchant for precision in surprising and seemingly insignificant areas. Studying these contradictory features with an aim to synthesize them with the tool marks he left behind fills out the complex picture of Fisher as a furniture maker.

Continued on page 130

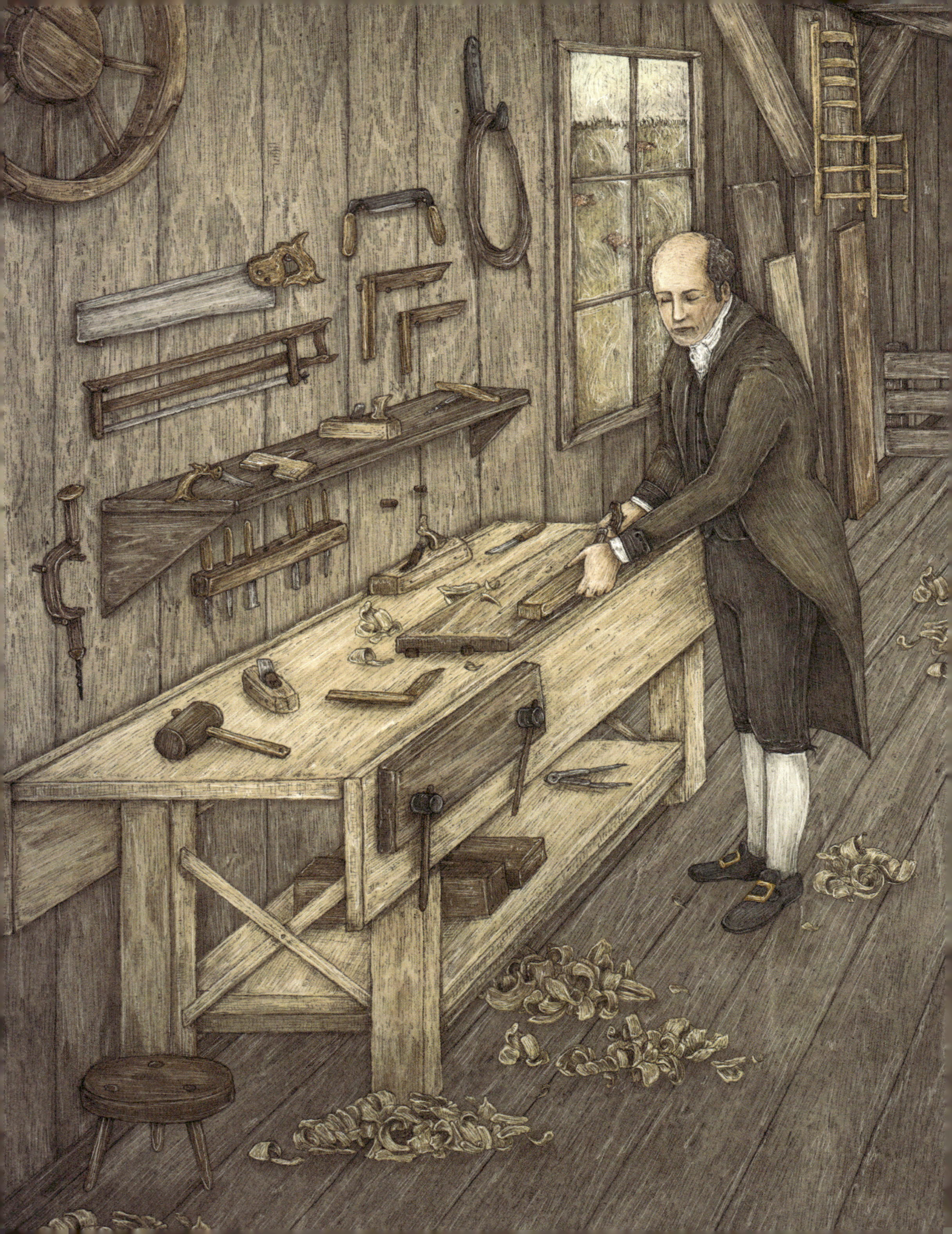

This image was commissioned to recreate Jonathan Fisher's workshop. The artist, Jessica Roux, relied on numerous photographs of the barn, Fisher's self-portrait, and tool and furniture artifacts.

Shop-based Research

Robert Tarule wrote: "It is possible to do history in the shop" and described the workshop as a "research tool and even a laboratory."[4] I have found this "shop-based research" to be an important way to understand the pre-industrial artisan's work. By recreating the process by which these objects were made, with the same methods and tools, a depth of understanding can be reached that cannot be gained by probate records or journal entries alone. As Tarule put it, "my work in the shop, and the questions it raised, helped form the questions I asked of the written documents."

During my years of research for the book, I applied Tarule's methodology to a few objects from the Fisher collection. Although many of my interpretations in the book are informed by shop-based research, the following are a few specific reflections on lessons learned through this process.

Hand Tools & the Economy of Labor

Even if the researcher/craftsman does not replicate a specific object exactly, having general experience using pre-industrial (hand-tool-only) methods can be an immense aid to interpretation. When I began this research in 2013, I was just about weaned off of woodworking machinery. As I became more comfortable tackling new shop situations without power tools, my understanding of Fisher's work increased greatly. The same conundrums he encountered, I encountered. As I explored deeper, Fisher's logic in construction (usually) began to make sense.

Although Fisher enjoyed his work, he, like other pre-industrial artisans, was not in it for the "Zen" moments of planing wood. This becomes obvious when looking at the guts of his furniture. These secondary surfaces reveal what Myrna Kaye has called the "economy of labor."[5] Things are not pretty under there. You find significant tear-out from the fore plane, glue squeeze-out and even sash-sawn mill marks. In 18th- and 19th-century America, this manner of work was not considered poor or sloppy workmanship. It was simply not worth the time to refine surfaces that wouldn't be seen. This kind of workmanship was simply par for the course.

As I've explored hand tools in my own shop and examined many examples of period workmanship, I have found that the key to efficiency is embracing the hand-tool textures. Rather than shying away from them, I've accepted them as evidence of the process in the same way the fingerprints of a potter may be left behind on a bowl or mug. Even though this "Wabi-sabi"-type aesthetic was not part of the consciousness of pre-industrial artisans, I've found that our own 21st-century fascination with "handmade" and "artisanal" objects aligns with the rawness of this honest texture.

Not Reinventing the Wheel

During my time studying Fisher's work, I've discovered the value in relying on stock profiles and motifs (and not just because it is a help to researchers for attribution, which it is). As much as Fisher was an artist when he approached the canvas, his furniture making relied mostly on time-tested telltale details: a beaded edge, his signature wooden knobs, and the creative combination of the same three molding planes. For woodworkers whose primary objective is unfettered artistic expression, having only three profiles might seem monotonous. But, for the pre-industrial artisan, being able to produce consistently successful work without reinventing the wheel was an asset. With three planes – an ogee, ovolo, and astragal with cove – Fisher successfully explored virtually every arrangement possible. I think he managed to display a strong unity to his work while avoiding monotony.

Even for woodworkers who do not rely on furniture making to feed their families, I think we can learn from this wisdom. I have found immense satisfaction in embracing my heritage by adopting some of its decorative customs. It's a tip of the hat. It acknowledges that I am part of a legacy of makers whose origin runs much deeper than my own. It is an incredible feeling to be a part of something bigger than myself.

Whether you choose time-tested details or blaze your own trail, I think it's worth pointing out that consciously reiterating your own signature characteristics in everything you make imparts a unity to your work. It is refreshing to walk into Fisher's house and see his fingerprints all over.

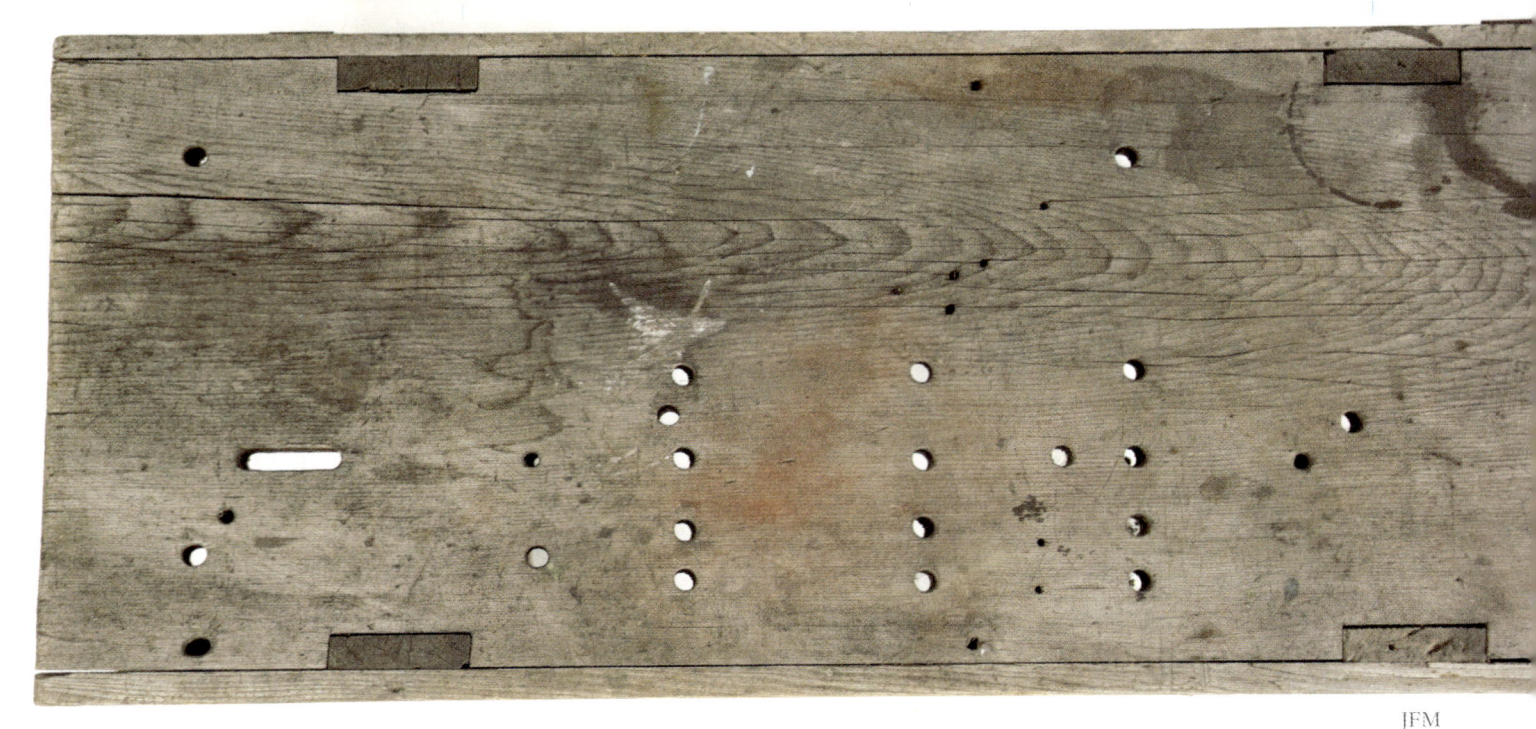

Nuremberg-pattern Peg Holes

Fisher's only surviving cabinetmaker's bench has a system of 5/8" peg holes that I have found effective for planing stock. This method of face planing is illustrated in a 1425 portrait of a Nuremberg joiner. The system has two parts: two stops at the end and the rows of holes 2" apart spaced every 6" down the length of the bench. The board can be held in place with four pegs installed, locking it in from two directions. The two pegs supporting the back of the board prevent lateral movement and the two at the end prevent it from moving forward. The result is stability in both directions for whatever kind of planing is necessary. This workholding system might be one of the most significant discoveries in the course of this research. Simple and effective, it is surprising we don't see its widespread use today. For those who are familiar with the "doe's foot" batten that prevents lateral movement while planing, the advantage of this system should be apparent; it has more support and is much easier to set up.

I bored this hole pattern in one of my workbench tops and, after experimenting with it a bit, I quite like it. The two pegs at the end are friction-fit and are adjusted much like a regular planing stop (by tapping with a mallet) but the third and fourth pegs have an intentional taper, swelling thicker at the very end to prevent them from dropping through. The pegs are trimmed low enough to remain shy of most stock thicknesses but are still easy to pull up with your fingers. This way, I can quickly lift the peg out of the hole and adjust it in a heartbeat, no mallet required. My pegs are made of soft pine to minimize the chance of denting the stock.

One of the trickier workholding needs woodworkers encounter is for planing across the grain (sometimes called "traversing"). Usually a batten or a doe's foot is used with holdfasts to secure the board against moving across the bench. The "Nuremberg" system makes this situation a breeze: Drop two pegs into the far holes and you can plane all day long. Genius.

I wish there were more to say about this method of workholding but it is forehead-slappingly simple. The advantages are not only economical (no fancy hardware to buy), they are practical. I've found this "Nuremberg" system to be the fastest way to adjust workholding besides using a lone planing stop. But the lateral support this one provides is worth seriously considering. It can easily be added to an existing bench with a toothed planing stop. All one would have to do is drill a line of holes 2" apart every 6" down the length of the bench. You don't need to make your bench Swiss cheese, though. Fisher only added the holes for the size of stock he knew he would be working with. I love this workholding system and can wholeheartedly commend it to you for your shop practice.

Stadtbibliothek im Bildungscampus Nürnberg,
Amb.317.2°,f.21r.

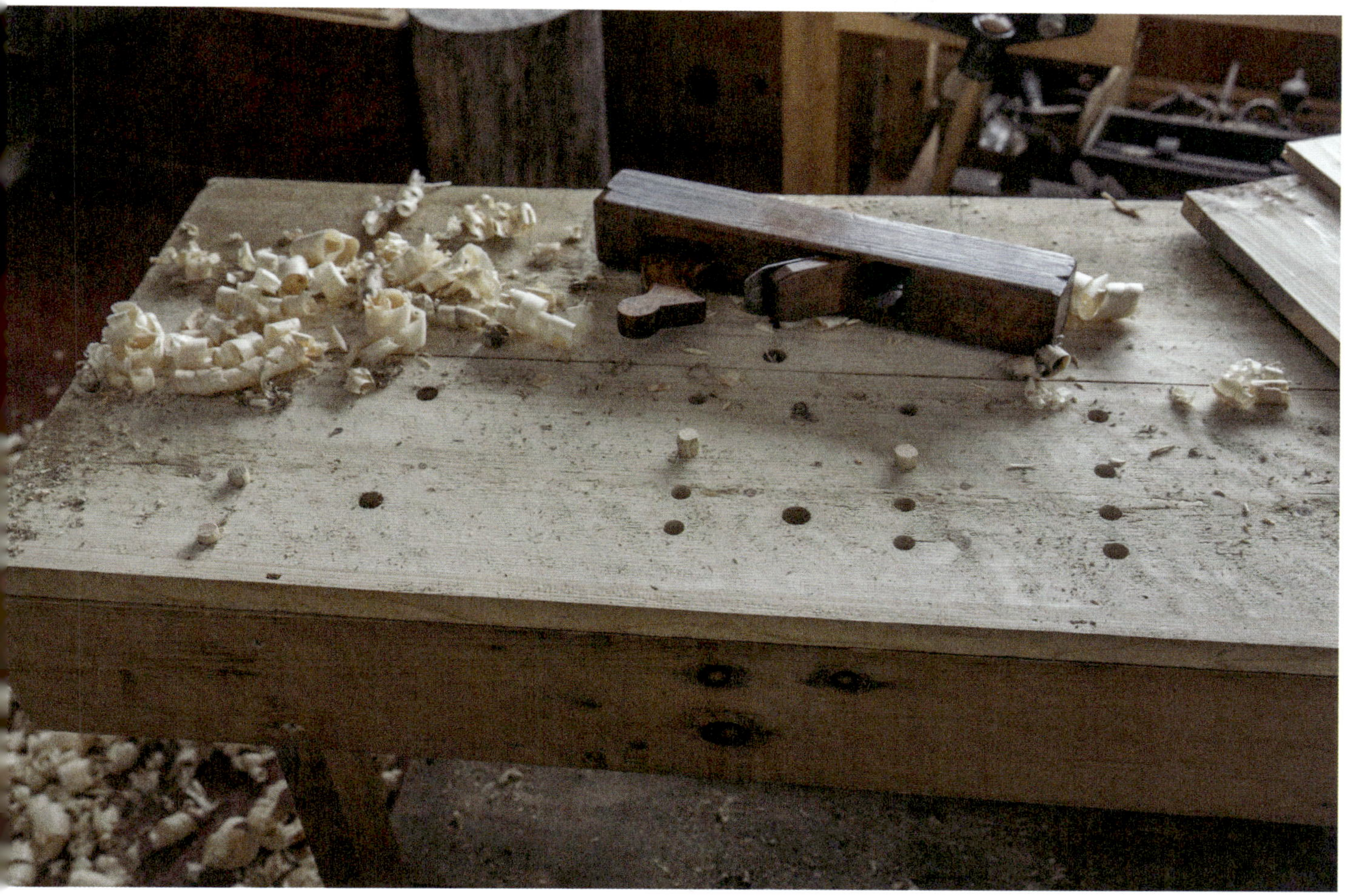

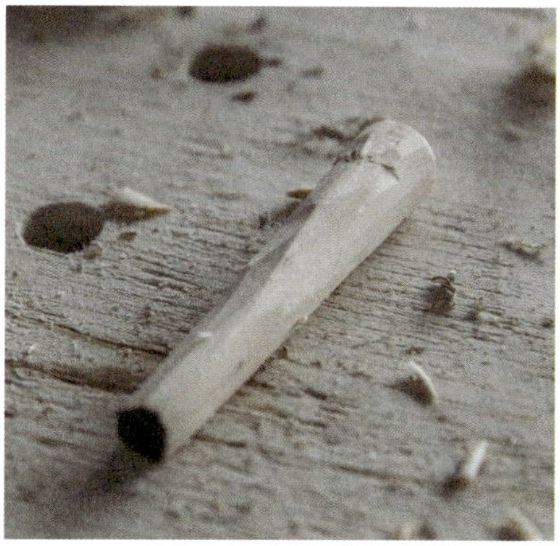

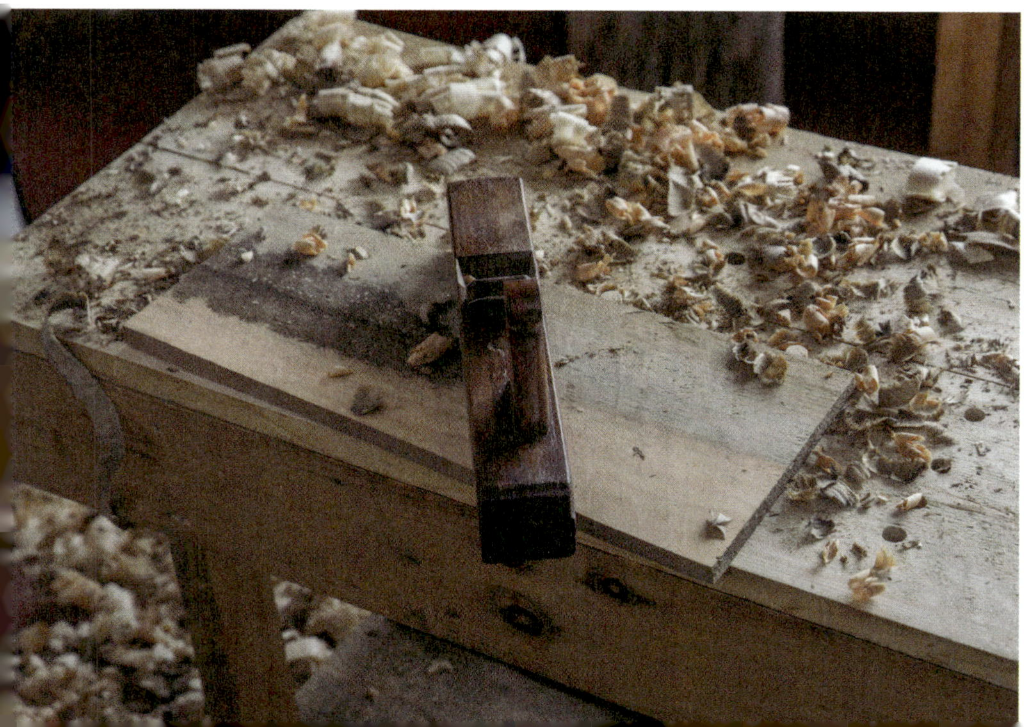

FM

Fisher's Tote

Before I saw Fisher's tools at the Farnsworth Museum, there were many pieces to the puzzle that didn't make sense. One of the most confounding was a small softwood pattern for laying out an unrecognizable shape (shown above, actual size). I took it around Fisher's house multiple times and held it up to the furniture, looking for some hint to what the pattern was for.

That first time I saw all of Fisher's tools spread out at the Farnsworth Museum, however, I was shocked to see that pattern over and over. It was the pattern for his handplane totes – a quirky, mouse-shaped tote.

The first time I saw the tote shape I assumed it was his own invention but I learned this style was used by a small number of other New England planemakers, though surviving examples are rare. The tote is referred to as a "Mickey Mouse" tote by plane collectors and is seen by some as idiosyncratic. I was unsure why Fisher would choose this pattern. Did he have tiny hands and need a small tote? Why was it so squat? And why wasn't the tote centered in the body like the 19th-century planes I use in my shop?

As I examined these tools, I was struck by how uncomfortable the shape seemed. It is wide at the base and flat – not rounded on its corners as is the more conventional style. I wondered how a person with small hands could wrap his or her hands around its huge base. I had to know. This was something I had to try for myself.

I replicated Fisher's tote shape and installed it on the body of an old dilapidated fore plane I had kicking around. I had no idea what to expect because looking at an object is worlds apart from using it. While planing boards, I ignored the plane and worked intuitively, switching between my usual fore plane and the modified one. I immediately saw the advantages of this odd tote. It felt radically different, and it wasn't until I looked down that I saw why. I had unconsciously allowed my pinky to slip down onto the sidewall of the plane (something not natural on a centered tote) because there was no room for a three-finger grip. I also had my index finger pointing forward in the direction I was planing, leaving only my middle and ring fingers wrapping around the tote front. This position slightly lowered my hand's center of gravity, putting more momentum behind the plane while at the same time allowing me to grab more of the plane than just the tote – similar to the small totes on Dutch planes. The combined effect made the plane feel more like a continuation of my arm (just like every great tool ought to). This grip position also explains the wideness at the base and the potentially uncomfortable lack of roundness: It was never the intention to grab it all the way around.

So what do I think having tried it? Is it awkward? Is the difference negligible? The answer is, I think this tote is amazing. As I moved back and forth between the two fore planes, I was struck by how the conventional tote seemed almost awkward in comparison. Having your pinky bracing the side of the plane gives a stabilizing effect, almost the way a tripod is more stable than a monopod. I am thankful to have a plane with this offset "mouse" tote. If you are making your own planes or are going to commission one from a planemaker, I highly recommend you give it a shot. It's changing my work for the better.

JFM

Conclusion

The survival of the Fisher story gives us a rare glimpse into the life of an 18th- and early 19th-century craftsman. There are very few collections of pre-industrial furniture makers so complete. Not only can we analyze his tools and study the furniture he built, but his mind and heart are laid bare for us in the countless journals and letters he left behind. This kind of three-dimensional look at the man makes history come alive for us. In Fisher's surviving furniture, we see the fingerprints of a passionate and creative artist doing what it takes to make ends meet. His singular vision to honor God in fulfilling his calling was inextricably woven into the fabric of his creative work. He delighted in details but avoided pretense. And Fisher was honest about his mistakes. The humble and solid furniture that stands centuries later is a fitting emblem for the man himself.

Spending time immersed in this refreshingly transparent story is an encouragement to me as a woodworker. It is easy to decontextualize and romanticize pre-industrial furniture making until we perceive the standards of craftsmanship to be so far out of reach that they paralyze us at the bench. In moments like these, we need perspective. The furniture of Fisher is the essential antidote. I hope his work encourages you to take pride in the work of your hands.

Interacting with Fisher's body of work has affected me profoundly. Through using tools such as he used and building the way he built, the strange world of Fisher has become a little more familiar than I thought possible. I've learned to take delight in honest hard work and am no longer ashamed of the tool marks that attest to it. During moments spent surveying a piece that I've made, every plane track and every saw cut brings me back to that moment of creation. It causes me to reflect as Fisher did, "Hands, what a blessing they are when employed aright." ◆

ENDNOTES

1. Kevin D. Murphy, *Jonathan Fisher of Blue Hill, Maine: Commerce, Culture, and Community on the Eastern Frontier* (Amherst and Boston: University of Massachusetts Press, 2010), 3.
2. Letter to Ashby from Fisher, October 26, 1795.
3. Samuel B. Harding, *The Contest over the Ratification of the Federal Constitution in the State of Massachusetts* (New York: Longmans-Green, 1896), 8, quoted in Ronald F. Banks, *Maine Becomes a State: The Movement to Separate Maine from Massachusetts, 1785-1820* (New Hampshire Publishing Co.; Wesleyan/Maine Historical Society, 1973), 9.
4. Robert Tarule, *The Artisan of Ipswich: Craftsman and Community in Colonial New England* (Baltimore: Johns Hopkins University Press, 2010), 135.
5. Myrna Kaye, *Fake, Fraud, or Genuine? Identifying Authentic American Antique Furniture* (Boston, New York, London: Bulfinch Press, 1991)

JFM

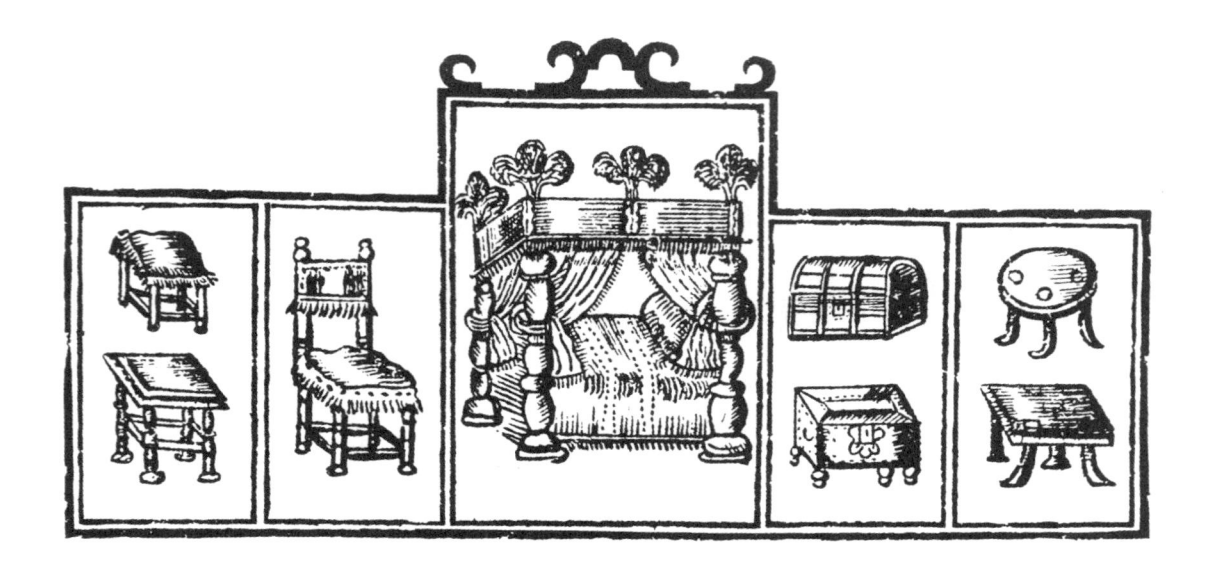

OAK FURNITURE
The * British * Tradition

A History of Early Furniture in the British Isles and New England

Victor Chinnery

Oak Furniture: The British Tradition. By Victor Chinnery. Antique Collectors Club; Revised Edition. 2016. 552 pages.

Reviewed by Derek Olson

It only takes a few years of reading standard woodworking literature to become disenchanted with the stock rotation of how-tos and "essential tricks." While helpful for beginners, most craftspeople eventually grow out of these resources. Once they get experience under their belts, they want something that treats them like an adult and expands their concept of form and function.

I've always found this inspiration in the older books referenced in bibliographies and footnotes. One of the greatest gems I've discovered is Victor Chinnery's *Oak Furniture: The British Tradition*. Ever since I got a copy of the original edition, I've been evangelizing anyone who will listen.

Oak Furniture is important because it shows us many interesting paths – joinery, marquetry, scratch-stock profiles, carving details, painted finishes, and much more. This book is rife with brief mentions of such things as lining boxes with woodcut printed papers – something I've found valuable in my own work. When I need inspiration, I find it in Chinnery.

But I'm not alone in my love for this book – it has also influenced the work of other modern makers. It was an invaluable resource for Jennie Alexander and Peter Follansbee's research into 17th-century American furniture, and Christopher Schwarz has several times mentioned his reliance on *Oak Furniture* during his exploration of vernacular forms. It's almost as if Chinnery is a furniture-making Rorschach Test, with different people divining individual inspiration based on who they are and why they're looking.

The book covers a lot of material. It begins with historical context, offering an overview of the evolution of trades, guild systems, and lives of the craftsmen. This is followed by a section that takes furniture out of the sterile study and speaks to its role in the historic household.

The second chapter illustrates the role of the makers in production. Chinnery describes the workshop and work conditions of several related trades before delving into a discussion of their preferred wood species and methods of decoration.

The third chapter is the real meat of Chinnery's work – nearly 200 pages of photographs and discussion of different furniture forms. He shows us everything from the simplest designs found in the average household to the highest-end works made for the upper crust. He explains the stylistic progression that influenced the look of this furniture and ends the chapter with an important discussion of terminology.

The final section breaks down the evolution of style and forms through chronological and regional influences. Best of all, this chapter offers even more photographic inspiration demonstrating the many ways furniture solves two basic problems: 1) how to suspend a platform off the floor (tables and chairs) and 2) how to store and protect important things (boxes, chests, and cupboards).

The six appendices are a nice punctuation, with excerpts from difficult-to-find historical volumes, several period probate lists, and notes on furniture scholarship and collections leading up to this work. Although the focus of this study is British furniture, Colonial American sources are relied upon, and there are plenty of breadcrumbs leading to France, Italy, and other European nations.

If there's a drawback to this book it's that it is too massive. Reading it straight through is like attempting to read the Bible cover to cover – Chinnery is best taken in bite-sized chunks. I suggest you let the stories, concepts, and forms settle before coming back for more. In fact, it may just be this book's massiveness that allows it to give up something new every time the cover is cracked. Chinnery doesn't foist upon his reader a pre-determined path as if this were a "how-to" book. Rather, like the best teachers, he shows you many doorways so that you can choose your own adventure.

Seventeenth-century scholar Robert Burton wrote, "A dwarf standing on the shoulders of a giant may see farther than the giant himself." *Oak Furniture* is one of my giants. This book is a conduit to correspondence with the past that offers invaluable inspiration for our work in the present. It will move you beyond popular media tedium by expanding your ideas about what constitutes good work, good furniture, and good design. Chinnery won't answer all your questions, but he will help you ask better ones. I believe that's much more important. ◆

SPONSOR DIRECTORY

The following are the businesses and individuals that sponsor this edition of *Mortise & Tenon Magazine*. This Directory is a way to highlight the mutual endorsement we share with our sponsors. The bottom line is: if someone is listed here it's because we support what they're doing and they support what we're doing. Everyone in this Directory has been hand-selected for high-quality and high-integrity business practice. These folks share our vision to celebrate historic furniture making and offer tools, training, and inspiration to aid your creative life.

If you are looking for recommendations of suppliers or makers, we recommend you look here first. We happily endorse and support these companies and hope you will, too.

Benchcrafted
Fine Vises & Tools

Fine vises for traditional workbenches, bench appliances from the golden age of woodworking, and unique tools for the modern hand tool enthusiast. Entirely made in the US of A.

www.benchcrafted.com
info@benchcrafted.com

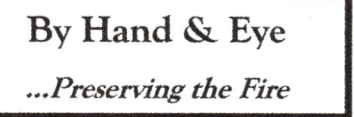

Blackburn Tools

Blackburn Tools is dedicated to the craft and art of saws and other handtools, and furnishes tools and support to woodworkers interested in the same. Focused on saw parts and kits, with comprehensive saw building instructions and resources freely available on our website.

blackburntools.com
isaac@blackburntools.com

Blue Spruce Toolworks
Hand tools for your finest work

We started Blue Spruce Toolworks with a singular vision: Hand crafted tools that are not only aesthetically beautiful, but are also a joy to use in the creative process. It is our hope that our tools - like the pieces you create with them - will be passed down and enjoyed for generations to come.

www.bluesprucetoolworks.com

By Hand & Eye
...Preserving the Fire

The design language of the ancient artisans united their skill set with the simple, harmonic proportions they observed in nature. Join Jim Tolpin & George Walker in their on-line "Designer's Atelier" to learn this timeless language of the artisans.

www.byhandandeye.com

Charleston Woodworking School

The Charleston Woodworking School offers a blend of traditional skills & contemporary techniques producing quality furniture. Marquetry, gilding, joinery, design, restoration and more are faculty taught with the Professional Course, Continuing Education and Short Courses. VA benefits approved.

www.charlestonwoodworkingschool.com

The Colonial Homestead

The Colonial Homestead offers one of the nation's finest selections of handtools, period furniture, and artisan work. In 2017, we are adding a trade school (Colonial Homestead Artisans Guild). With over 11,000 square feet of handtools, workshop, antiques, artisanwork, fine art, and handtool classes, Colonial Homestead is a one-stop destination.

www.cohoartguild.com
330-600-9445

ETWAS Warranted U.S.A.

Makers of fine tool bags and custom leather cases. Proud to use the best US made and naturally vegetable tanned leather and solid metal fittings. Individually hand sewn in Vermont, USA.

www.etwasbags.com

Fine Tool Journal

The *Fine Tool Journal* is a quarterly magazine for the user and avid collector of fine hand tools, including articles on tool history, use, and preservation. Each issue also features an absentee auction with choice selections of user and collectible hand tools.

www.finetooljournal.net
finetoolj@gmail.com

Fine WoodWorking

For over 40 years, *Fine Woodworking* has been providing the most trusted and highest quality information on every aspect of the woodworking craft. Experienced and respected woodworkers share their extensive knowledge with an audience of all skill levels, whether they are novices or advanced woodworkers building the most challenging projects.

www.finewoodworking.com

Furniture Institute of Massachusetts

The Furniture Institute of Massachusetts is dedicated to excellence in the art of classical woodworking techniques and functional contemporary furniture design and construction. We have a program designed to teach the traditional woodworking techniques that have for centuries proven successful in building the world's masterpieces. Full-time, nights, weekends & summer programs available.

http://www.furnituremakingclasses.com

Grandpa's Little Farm
~Reconditioned Vintage Handtools~

Tool restoration was just part of a small hobby farm that we started in 2009. We specialize in user woodworking tools, specializing in braces, bits, and metal bodied planes, but will try to track down special items on request. We take pride in spending time with each client and completely warranty each item we ship. And coming soon will be our own product line of apparel and tool care items!

www.grandpaslittlefarm.com   253-536-0197

Highland Woodworking
Fine Tools since 1978

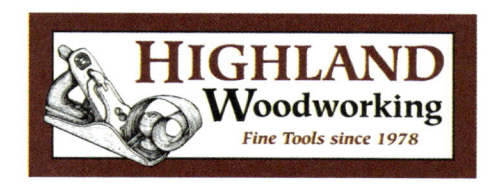

A family-owned business, Highland Woodworking has served woodworkers with fine tools and education since 1978. Always committed to quality and value, Highland is well known for providing reliable advice on the purchase and use of woodworking tools.

http://www.highlandwoodworking.com
(800) 241-6748

HORTON BRASSES, INC.

Since 1936, Horton Brasses has been making period correct reproduction hardware. Our patterns are exact copies of antique originals and we employ traditional production methods wherever possible. The addition of the Londonderry Brasses collection means we have more selection and capability than ever before.

www.horton-brasses.com

Lee Valley & Veritas

Lee Valley and Veritas® are Canadian family-owned businesses that have been supplying high quality woodworking, gardening, and home products since 1978.

http://leevalley.com
1- 800-267-8735

LIBERTY TOOL COMPANY / DAVISTOWN MUSEUM

The Liberty Tool Co. is the largest branch of the Jonesport Wood Company, which also has locations in Hulls Cove (The Tool Barn) and Searsport (Captain Tinkham's Emporium). The Davistown Museum is a regional tool, art, and history museum that chronicles tools and the impact they have on the individuals and societies using them.

http://www.libertytoolco.com
http://davistownmuseum.org   (207) 589-4771

Lie-Nielsen TOOLWORKS INC.

Our Mission is to design and create beautiful heirloom-quality hand tools that inspire woodworkers and other artisans. Through exceptional support and education, our customers receive the same personal attention we put into our tools.

http://lie-nielsen.com
(800) 327-2520

the MAINE COAST CRAFT SCHOOL

Offering classes in traditional green wood working at our off-the-grid, hand-built school in Bristol, Maine. We teach spoons, bowls, chairs, baskets, knife & sheath making, edge tool sharpening, coopering. Distributors of Hans Karlsson, Svante Djärv & USA-made tools for working green wood.

www.mainecoastcraft.com

Mary May's School of Traditional Woodcarving

My online video school teaches a variety of traditional woodcarving techniques, focusing on period furniture details and classical ornamentation. To keep the instruction fresh and unique, a new HD video is added every week.

http://www.marymaycarving.com/carvingschool
(843) 200-9469

Michael Mascelli UPHOLSTERER

Specialist in period upholstery treatments using traditional materials and techniques; hybrid and minimally intrusive treatments for both new and heirloom pieces. Classes in upholstery offered at Marc Adams School of Woodworking and Connecticut Valley School of Woodworking and by appointment.

threadclips@juno.com
518-785-9391

M-WTCA

Studying, Preserving, and Sharing Knowledge of Tools

Please check out our website for information and to join. Our meetings are one of the best places to find the hand tools you are looking for, as well as folks who know the history behind them.

www.MWTCA.org

NORTH BENNET ST. SCHOOL
AN EDUCATION IN CRAFTSMANSHIP

A life of proven skills, artful solutions, and superior craftsmanship – built by hand. Full-Time programs and Continuing Education classes in furniture making and fine woodworking. Master faculty and an inspiring community located in Boston's historic North End. Financial aid and veterans' benefits available.

http://nbss.edu/furniture
617.227.0155

NORTH HOUSE FOLK SCHOOL
ENRICHING LIVES & BUILDING COMMUNITY THROUGH TRADITIONAL NORTHERN CRAFT

North House is an educational non-profit located on the shore of Lake Superior in Minnesota. Our mission is to enrich lives and build community by teaching traditional northern crafts in a student-centered learning environment that inspires the hands, the heart and the mind. Furniture building, woodturning and beyond.

www.northhouse.org
218-387-9762

Plate 11 Workbench Co.

Plate 11 Woodworking makes and teaches classes on making Roubo workbenches, tool chests, shave horses and any other piece of woodwork you see on their Instagram feed (@markbuildsit).

http://www.plate11.com

POPULAR Woodworking

Learn How. Discover Why. Build Better. Through our magazine, books, videos, and more, *Popular Woodworking* inspires and educates furniture makers of all skill levels with a broad range of historical and contemporary tool and technique instruction, projects and more, from some of today's best-known woodworkers.

http://popularwoodworking.com/
popwood@fwmedia.com